A BETTER CLASS OF PERSON
and
GOD ROT TUNBRIDGE WELLS

A BETTER CLASS OF PERSON
OF PERSON
[An Extract of Autobiography for Television]

and

GOD ROT
TUNBRIDGE WELLS

by

JOHN OSBORNE

faber and faber
LONDON · BOSTON

First published in 1985
by Faber and Faber Limited
3 Queen Square London WC1N 3AU

Photoset and Printed in Great Britain by
Redwood Burn Limited
Trowbridge Wiltshire

R00480 36469

British Library Cataloguing in Publication Data

Osborne, John, *1929*—
A better class of person; and, God rot Tunbridge Wells.
I. Title
II. Osborne, John, *1929*—. God rot Tunbridge Wells.
822'.914   PR6029.S39
ISBN 0-571-13127-1

A BETTER CLASS
OF PERSON

CHARACTERS

JOHN
MRS OSBORNE
MR OSBORNE
MICKEY
LADY ALMONER
ISABEL
RAYMOND
ISABEL'S MOTHER
ISABEL'S GRANDMOTHER
NURSE at sanatorium
GRANDAD OSBORNE
EDNA
MRS WILLIAMS
WOMAN (with coal bunker)
HEADMASTER (Chadacre School)

BOY (Chadacre School)
TEACHER (Chadacre School)
NEWSAGENT
GRANDAD GROVE
GRANDMA GROVE
NURSE ATKINS
WATSON (Country School)
PREFECT (Country School)
HEADMASTER (Country School)
JENNY
AMERICAN SAILOR
ERIC
MASTER (Country School)
CLERGYMAN (Crematorium)

Policeman
The Jolly Dinkies
People on Bognor Pier
Whelk Stall Man
Air Raid Warden
Policemen
Pub Cellar crowd
2 Stretcher Men
Commissionaire
Old Man in Waiting Room
2 Ambulance Men
Removal Men
Doctor
Schools Attendance Officer
Sanatorium Patients
Sanatorium Nurses
Sanatorium Uniform Men (2)
Woman Teacher
Boys & Girls
Lots of children in School Hall

Children in class
Teachers
Pupils
Firemen
Organist
People in cinema
People at Station (Country)
Matron
Clergyman
Boys in Convalescent Home
Servicemen (Waterloo Station)
Boys & Parents (Waterloo
    Station)
Sailor (carriage)
Boys in Boarding School
Girl playing tennis
Piano Teacher
Exam Room Teacher
People in Pub

A Better Class of Person was first transmitted by Thames Television in June 1985. The cast included:

MR OSBORNE	Alan Howard
MRS OSBORNE	Eileen Atkins
YOUNG JOHN	Gary Capelin
OLDER JOHN	Neil McPherson
YOUNGER MICKEY	Justin Kielty
OLDER MICKEY	David Garlick
LADY ALMONER	Richenda Carey
ISABEL	Sophie Ward
RAYMOND	Spencer Banks
ISABEL'S MOTHER	June Marlow
ISABEL'S GRANDMOTHER	Peggy Aitchison
DOCTOR	Gerald Bryce
GRANDAD OSBORNE	Roger Milner
MRS WILLIAMS	Shirley Stelfox
HEADMASTER, Chadacre School	John Grillo
BOY, Chadacre School	Matthew Duke
TEACHER, Chadacre School	William Simons
GRANDAD GROVE	Derek Smith
GRANDMA GROVE	Julia McCarthy
NURSE ATKINS	Patricia Heneghan
WATSON, Country School	Mark Rogers
PREFECT, Country School	Daniel Beales
HEADMASTER, Country School	Tim Seely
JENNY (Head's Niece)	Jenna Russell
AMERICAN SAILOR	Kenny Andrews
ERIC	Rio Fanning
MASTER, Country School	John Barrard
CLERGYMAN at crematorium	Seymour Green
WOMAN (with Coal Bunker)	Barbara Keogh
THE JOLLY DINKIES	The Beaux Bells

Produced and Directed by Frank Cvitanovich
Designed by David Marshall and Robin Parker

1. EXT. STREET. DAY
A long, steep hill. It is almost rural but the traces of incipient suburbia are upon it. It is deserted, quite still. In the far distance a single figure can be seen making a slow advance up the hill. Presently it can be seen to be a POLICEMAN. *He is on a bicycle and wearing a blue tin helmet. At this stage, he is little more than a stick figure. Slowly he makes his almost painful but determined progress up the empty street. Silence. His outline becomes clear and we see that he has a gas-mask case flapping against him and that there is a placard hanging round his neck. He is an almost comic figure, like a stock village policeman from a film of the period.*

2. EXT. STREET. DAY
A window above a small 1930s shopping arcade. A SMALL BOY *is staring out into the street.*

3. EXT. STREET. DAY
The POLICEMAN *draws closer and closer. We see his face sweating.*

4. EXT. WINDOW. DAY
The SMALL BOY *stares down.*

5. EXT. STREET. DAY
The POLICEMAN. *Close-up of Placard:* TAKE COVER.

6. EXT. WINDOW. DAY
The SMALL BOY *looks up to the sky. Clear. Air-raid siren.*

7. ROSTRUM SHOT
Close-up of wartime identity card. The number on the front: EPHA 64 3.

8. INT. BEDROOM. DAY
The BOY *turns round.* BOY: Hey, Dad!

9. INT. BEDROOM. DAY.
A very frail grey-haired MAN *in his late thirties is lying in bed, his thin arms over the cover, clutching the* Sunday Express. *(Whatever*

11

the headline was – NO WAR? *That would be nice.) The room is fairly plain but with a few lower-middle-class odds and ends – not too obvious. But a china lady with borzois would not be going too far. An Ecko radio. An older-looking woman in overalls comes in from the nearby kitchen with a dishcloth. It is his* MOTHER.

FATHER: Quiet, son.

MOTHER: Yes, hold your bloody noise. Your father's upset. Can't you see that? And go and open my Guinness.

BOY: But Mum, it's an air raid –

MOTHER: Oh, I don't know what it is. My dinner's burning. Bloody Germans! Why do they always want to go fighting? And turn that bloody wireless off.
(*The* BOY *goes into the kitchen.*)
Thank God you're no good to them yet anyway.

FATHER: No.

MOTHER: They say it'll all be over by Christmas.

FATHER: There's him . . .

MOTHER: Who'd ever want *him*? Fat lot of good . . .

10. INT. KITCHEN. DAY

The BOY *opens a bottle at the sink. As he does so, pouring into a glass, he looks out at the sky.*

ROBB WILTON: (*Voice over*) 'The day war broke out, the missus said to me . . .'

11. ROSTRUM SHOT

Close-up. The identity card opens. Inside is written: JOHN JAMES OSBORNE, EPHA 64 3.

12. EXT. ROCK POOL. DAY

Slimy green rock. The tide cascades into the pool, turning it into a little bubbling reservoir, then recedes, leaving it a whirl of sand and weed settling back into still, dark, clear water. A few tiny crabs scurry away over the sides, leaving others hiding in dark crevices.

JOHN OSBORNE: (*Voice over*) Identity: identity of childhood often seems more defined than recent pleasure or grief. A delusion perhaps, but an attempt to salvage some *thing* of the derelict past. So that one can say: I *was* there . . .

Instead of where am I now? Among ravages of present
turmoil...

13. EXT. ROCK POOL. DAY
*Close-up of crabs and small fish in the pool. After the miniscule
explosion, it is very still. Flashes of watery sunlight and wriggling
sand. Still, like being in a tunnel, remote, protected. Muffled sea
sounds crashing against a blanket of rocks.*
JOHN OSBORNE: (*Voice over*) But I do remember. *So* well.
    Better than last year. What *did* happen then? Or three. Five
    years ago. I don't think I am inventing it for myself. Or,
    indeed, anyone else. I'm sure... A time comes when the
    slime can be safely scraped away.

14. EXT. ROCK POOL. DAY
*A bucket and spade. A small hand pokes in among the sand and the
water clouds over into another little storm.*

15. EXT. ROCK POOL. DAY
The BOY *staring intently into the pool.*
JOHN OSBORNE: (*Voice over*) The tide recedes a long way before
    being allowed to return... Trickling into the still-stranded
    pools.

16. EXT. ROCK POOL. DAY
The BOY *stands up and looks out at the sea crashing against the rock
and creating more bubbling reservoirs around him. Wet, crinkled
sand and pebbles.*
JOHN OSBORNE: (*Voice over*) When it has finally entered into
    the blood and softening bone of a lifetime.

17. EXT. LONG SWEEP OF BEACH. DAY
The BOY *clambers over the rocks. Towards the sea. In the distance a
few isolated deckchairs but, on the whole, a fairly empty landscape.*
JOHN OSBORNE: (*Voice over*) I *know* that the summer of 1939
    was beautiful. Just as 1914 was. Whatever official records
    may say. Not as bright and brilliant as 1940 was to be with
    its brilliant flashes of aircraft wings spluttering over endless
    blue skies.

18. ROSTRUM SHOTS
Period-postcard views of Bognor Regis.
JOHN OSBORNE: (*Voice over*) When I was born the First World
   War was still a raw memory of a mere dozen years. But
   now, to most of us, those summers before 1939 must seem
   as faint as August 1914. Not to me.

19. EXT. BOGNOR REGIS. DAY
*Shots of Bognor today. Places mentioned, including Stalag-Butlin
and prisoners.*
JOHN OSBORNE: (*Voice over*) Bognor Regis, immortalized by
   the late king. 'Bugger Bognor!' Were they really his last
   words? I hope so even if it was a little unfair. Last summer
   I took my daughter there. It seemed much the same.
   Tame? Perhaps, but unassuming and cheerful. The same
   arcade of shops, pier – now decapitated – a first-class
   bookshop, Queen Victoria's old hotel. Apart from a few
   concessions to fashion and dress, it could almost have been
   1938.

20. EXT. PIERHEAD PIERROT THEATRE. DAY
Masthead: BOGNOR JOLLY DINKIES OF 1938. *The* JOLLY
DINKIES, *accompanied by the piano, encourage the usual seaside
audience to join in appropriate 1938 favourites.* JOHN *and* MICKEY
watch.

21. EXT. PIER. DAY
JOHN *and* MICKEY *have a traditional good time, enjoying the
delights of the pier.*

22. EXT. PROMENADE. DAY
JOHN *and* MICKEY *gaze over the railings in silence.*

23. EXT. BEACH. EVENING
JOHN *and* MICKEY *running across the shadowy beach.*

24. EXT. BEACH. EVENING

JOHN *and* MICKEY *stare mournfully out to sea. The sun is going down as they turn up towards the prom. They turn and look again.*

MICKEY: Do you think they'll let us come next year?

JOHN: Don't know.

MICKEY: Don't suppose so.

JOHN: Bet we do! (*Shouting*) We'll be back. Next year! We'll be back. You see . . .

(*They pick up stones and hurl them into the sea.*)

25. EXT. SEA. EVENING

Pebbles ricochet over the waves. Thrown by skilled hands.

26. INT. BEDROOM. NIGHT

FATHER *is in bed reading a book.* JOHN *is lying on the floor. Beside him is a toy fort with soldiers. He is pinning flags with swastikas, British and French flags on to a map of Europe spread out on the floor in front of him.*

'CHAMBERLAIN': (*Voice over, a comic's cod version*) 'And no such undertaking having been received, this country is at a state of war with Germany.'

JOHN: Where's Danzig, Dad?

FATHER: Poland, I think. Or Germany.

JOHN: Do you think it *will* be over by Christmas?

FATHER: Shouldn't think so.

JOHN: That's good. Will we go to Grandma's for Christmas?

FATHER: Haven't thought.

JOHN: Did they really call Scottish soldiers the Ladies from Hell?

FATHER: Who?

JOHN: The Germans. And they were frightened to death of the Gurkhas – cut out their gizzards with knives – kooies. Mickey's father says they did terrible things to the Belgians. And they shot Nurse Cavell.

FATHER: I don't remember much about it. I wasn't much older than you. I got chased by a lot of women in 1916 when we lived in Southsea.

JOHN: What for?

FATHER: They had white feathers. They gave them to men who were cowards and wouldn't join up.

JOHN: But you were too young.

FATHER: I was tall for my age.

JOHN: Were you scared?

FATHER: Very.

JOHN: Would you have joined up?

FATHER: They wouldn't have had me . . .

JOHN: I think I'd go in the Navy.

FATHER: Well – it's in the family. Turn the wireless on, will you, son?

(JOHN *does so.*)

JOHN: Do you think I'll be able to go to Bognor next year with Mickey?

FATHER: Depends on Mickey's dad. And the Germans, I suppose.

MOTHER: (*Entering*) Stop talking to your father. You know it only fags him out. Then *I'm* the one who gets it.

FATHER: (*Winks at* JOHN.) We were discussing the war.

MOTHER: Well, turn that bloody wireless off then. On all day. Gets on my nerves.

27. EXT. BOGNOR BEACH. DAY
Summer 1940. Fortified beach with barbed wire and tank traps, pillboxes, etc. Wind blowing the sand across the notices: DANGER: MINES, *etc.*

28. EXT. BOGNOR PROMENADE. DAY
JOHN *and* MICKEY *stare out at the endless skein of barbed wire on the beach. They walk along aimlessly, passing boarded-up shops and the old amusement arcade with its few customers, placards proclaiming day trips to France and so on.*

29. EXT. WHELK STALL. DAY
JOHN *and* MICKEY *munch glumly from their plates.*

JOHN: Swiz . . .

MICKEY: Um.

JOHN: Do you think they'll land here?

MICKEY: Expect so.

JOHN: What – the Germans?

> (MICKEY *nods*. JOHN *brightens up*.)
>
> Do you think they'll come while we're here?

MICKEY: Sure.

JOHN: Cor . . . (*Sadly*) But we've only got six days . . . Still, they *might* come then.

MICKEY: Wouldn't be surprised.

JOHN: Really?

MICKEY: Really.

> (*They ponder. Look out to sea expectantly. Presently –*) How much you got?

JOHN: Why?

MICKEY: They've got *Pinocchio* in Chichester.

> (*Pause. It's an alternative to invasion that afternoon.*)

JOHN: OK. Let's go.

30. EXT. CINEMA. DAY

JOHN *and* MICKEY *are eating ham rolls, coming out of the cinema after watching* Pinocchio.

31. EXT. CHICHESTER. DAY

The High Street towards Market Cross. JOHN *and* MICKEY *look in the windows of closed antique shops.*

JOHN: I like the Fox best.

MICKEY: You would.

JOHN: Why?

MICKEY: You just would.

JOHN: But why? Go on – tell me. What's wrong with that?

> (*The air-raid siren sounds and they look up at the sky eagerly. Suddenly people appear in the street. Police whistles blow. Shouts:* Take cover, *etc. The cellar doors in the pavement outside a pub open miraculously like a trap in pantomime.*)

VOICE: (*Shouting*) Come down here! Don't just stand there gawping! Do you want to get killed?

> (*Still staring behind them at the sky, they reluctantly follow a crowd into the cellar and the heavy doors thud closed above them.*)

32. INT. PUB CELLAR. DAY.

JOHN *and* MICKEY *crouched by the barrels with a crowd of adults.*
They wait as the sound of approaching aircraft grows louder.
Silence. Then a shattering hiss. The barrels rattle and shake. An
explosion and everything moves and rolls.

33. INT. PUB CELLAR. DAY

Dust clears. Everything settles. The crowd moves. JOHN *and*
MICKEY *look at each other in wonder.*
JOHN: Cor . . .

34. INT. PUB CELLAR. DAY

It goes black. All-clear sounds. A shaft of bright light circles JOHN
and MICKEY *as the heavy cellar doors are rolled back to reveal the*
sky. They hesitate, then clamber up the steps.

35. EXT. HIGH STREET. DAY

JOHN *and* MICKEY *blink in the bright sun delightedly.*
MICKEY: Swiz!
JOHN: Swiz.
MICKEY: Never mind. We'll just get the bus back. Come on!
    (*They start running.*)
JOHN: I still liked the Fox –
MICKEY: What?
JOHN: 'Hi diddle dee dee – an actor's life for me. Hi diddle dee-
    i . . .'
    (*They sing, laughing and running for the bus.*)

36. INT. BROMPTON HOSPITAL. DAY

The waiting hall. With an OLD MAN, JOHN *and his* MOTHER
sitting on long monastic benches. Indeed, the whole place has a cold,
cloistered atmosphere. OLD COMMISSIONAIRE *on duty. A door*
opens and a rather grand YOUNG WOMAN *in an overall steps out*
briskly. The door is marked LADY ALMONER.
ALMONER : Mrs Osborne?
    (MRS OSBORNE *rises apologetically.*)
    In here, please.
    (MRS OSBORNE *pushes* JOHN *in the back.*)

MOTHER: Don't forget – if she speaks to you – you say 'Lady
   Almoner'.
   (*They go in.*)

37. INT. LADY ALMONER'S OFFICE. DAY
The LADY ALMONER *is looking at them like a benign magistrate.*
ALMONER: So you want to be a sailor?
JOHN: Yes, Miss. Lady –
ALMONER: Why do you want to be a sailor?
JOHN: I don't know.
ALMONER: You'll have to eat a bit more if you're going to be a
   sailor. Anyway, I don't suppose it will come to that. Let's
   hope not. Now, Mrs Osborne, you do understand what this
   means, don't you?
MOTHER: I think so.
ALMONER: As you know, there's really nothing more we can do
   for your husband.
MOTHER: Yes, you've been very good.
ALMONER: Well, we can't perform miracles. And, with a war
   on, heaven knows what most other people will have to face,
   not just yourself . . . He hasn't been able to work much for
   the past few years of course. All these sanatoriums . . .
   Colindale. Yes. The benevolent society he belongs to seems
   to have been very generous. Very generous . . .
MOTHER: Everyone's been ever so kind.
ALMONER: The South of France didn't seem to be very
   successful. It must have been very expensive.
MOTHER: He didn't like the German nurses.
ALMONER: Yes. Well, we have to make do with what we can
   get in these things. He's been really rather lucky. In a *way*,
   of course. I believe the Isle of Wight can be very nice.
   Healthy air and, of course, it should be safer – away from
   the bombs.
MOTHER: I don't know whether he'll like going away.
ALMONER: (*Rising*) Well, I'm sure you'll manage. (*To* JOHN)
   You like the seaside, don't you?
   (*He nods.*)

19

Away from the war and the air raids. I'm sure you'll have a lovely time, making new friends. You'll probably see all the convoys going past your bedroom. (*Puts out her hand.*) Try not to worry, Mrs Osborne. You really are lucky, getting away from it. It's sure to get worse before it's over.

38. EXT. FIELD. DAY
JOHN and MICKEY *lie looking up at barrage balloons in the distance.*
MICKEY: How long will you be there?
JOHN: Till my dad gets better.
MICKEY: When will that be?
JOHN: Don't know. It's to get the air in his lungs. Wish we weren't going . . . She said we'd be getting away from the bombs.
(*He looks wistfully upwards.*)
MICKEY: Oh . . .
JOHN: We're going in the Daimler ambulance.
MICKEY: Cor.

39. EXT. FLAT OVER SHOP. DAY
John's FATHER *is being carried down the iron staircase on a stretcher to a waiting Daimler ambulance below.* JOHN *watches.*

40. EXT. AMBULANCE. DAY
The stretcher is lifted into the ambulance. JOHN *and his* MOTHER *follow. Door closed.*

41. EXT. AMBULANCE. DAY
Ambulance on a Hampshire road. JOHN *looks out at the countryside.*

42. EXT. PORTSMOUTH FERRY. DAY
Ambulance going down loading ramp to go on to the ferry. Army lorry in the background with an Army truck DRIVER *leaning against it.*

43. EXT. CRUISER. DAY
From JOHN's *point of view on the ferry as he looks up to the bows of a cruiser. Three or four* SAILORS *are leaning over the rail.*

44. EXT. FERRY. DAY
JOHN *sitting on the deck of the ferry, looking towards the sea and huddled up in his coat.*

45. EXT. RYDE PIER. DAY
The ambulance arrives on the Isle of Wight. It goes along Ryde Pier towards the camera.

46. EXT. SMALL COUNTRY ROAD. EVENING
The ambulance draws up outside a small 1930s house. A removal van is being unloaded outside. MOTHER *gets out.* FATHER *is unloaded on his stretcher.* JOHN *runs into the house.*

47. INT. HOUSE. EVENING
JOHN *rushes up the stairs into a small room. It is obviously his as he recognizes his own things.*

48. INT. BEDROOM. EVENING
JOHN *goes over to the window, thrusting it open. It looks out over a garden, leading to the cliffs, with a small orchard. He looks out to the sea. In the dull light he can see the lights of large ships in the distance.*

49. EXT. UNDER CLIFF. DAY
JOHN *walks beneath the cliff, picking his way among huge stones on the empty stretch of beach.*

50. EXT. UPPER CLIFF. EVENING
Swathed in scarf and balaclava helmet, JOHN *puts his head down against the bitter wind from the sea. No one in sight. Ahead of him are the lights of the house.*

51. INT. HOUSE. NIGHT

JOHN *opens the door and comes in. His* MOTHER *is sitting by the grate listening to the radio.*

MOTHER: Your tea's cold. Where have you been?

JOHN: Walk.

MOTHER: Walk! I've been worried stiff. Nothing to look at out there. Just fog, bloody fog. No one to talk to. Bloody dead and alive hole . . . Give me the trolley buses every time, air raids or no air raids.

JOHN: (*Putting down gas-mask case*) Where's Dad?

MOTHER: Where d'you think? Don't you go up there talking to him – he's tired. You'd better make some toast.
(*She hands him the toasting fork. He sits, holding it in front of the grate. He stares into the red glow. There is no light. Suddenly, the house, indeed the whole island, seems to rumble and shake.* JOHN *hurtles upstairs.*)

MOTHER: (*Out of vision, shouting*) Oh, my God. What's that! Mind the black-out! Mind the black-out. Dad! Dad!

52. INT. BEDROOM. NIGHT

JOHN *dashes to the window, flings back the curtains and looks out.*

53. EXT. INT. SEA/BEDROOM. NIGHT

From JOHN's *point of view: an enormous roar as the sea is lit up by gunfire. He watches transfixed.*

54. INT. BEDROOM. DAY

JOHN *is sitting at a small desk made out of orange boxes. It is very misty. Beyond the little orchard he can see little. He is writing a letter to Mickey.*

JOHN: (*Voice over*) 'Dear Mick, You should have been here yesterday. I wish you had been. I'd just come back from a walk. They kept saying I should be back at school . . . well, Dad doesn't. I think he'd rather I were here. I take him up cups of tea all day and we talk and we read to one another when he's not feeling too tired. Mum goes on about it but he tells me not to take any notice of her so I don't. Well, all of a sudden, I was making some toast and there was the biggest bang you've ever heard. The whole island shook. Everyone says it was the destroyers with the convoy shooting at submarines but Dad says it must have been a light cruiser at least. You've never heard anything like it . . .'

55. EXT. CLIFF TOP. DAY

JOHN *peering through binoculars.*

JOHN: (*Voice over*) 'I bet there's another one soon as the convoys go right past here all the time. Mum went all daft and more bad-tempered and keeps saying we should never have come here, no proper pubs or buses hardly ever. She's in her black moods all the time. It's very lonely here . . . I miss our games . . . but perhaps it won't be too bad after all. It's *bound* to happen again. The lady at the hotel lent me her husband's old binoculars from the last war. They're wizard. Except it's so foggy, there's not much to see most of the time . . .'

(*Coughing, retching sounds.*)

56. INT. STAIRS LANDING. DAY

JOHN *is taking up a tray of bread and butter and tea to his* FATHER *who can be seen and heard coughing in bed. He takes in the tray to him and puts a newspaper on the bed.*

57. INT. BEDROOM. DAY

JOHN *is reading his paper. His* FATHER *reads an old* Boy's Own Annual *as he sips his tea.* JOHN *cuts out a drawing from the paper and glues it into a large scrapbook.*

JOHN: (*Voice over*) 'Me and Dad talk about the war all the time. He got quite upset about the *Rawalpindi* being sunk. He used to know someone on the P. & O. There's a smashing drawing of it going down in the *Daily Mail*. I've cut it out and put it in my war book. I asked Dad what he wanted for Christmas and he said a book and gave me three to choose from: *Ariel* – it's all about Shelley – *A Safety Match* by Ian Hay or *Death of a Hero*. They're sixpence each so I might be able to get all three. What do you want for Christmas? I don't think I'll be able to send anything. Do you think the Germans will attack before then? Perhaps they won't bother to come here . . .'

58. INT. KITCHEN. DAY

JOHN *is sitting down at the table near to tears. His* MOTHER *is talking to a patient-looking* MAN *in a heavy raincoat and scarf with a briefcase. Presently a* MAN, *carrying a doctor's bag, comes down the stairs. The three adults talk as the boy looks on abjectly. Then he dashes up the stairs to his father's room. We see* FATHER *through the door, his eyes barely open, exhausted.*

JOHN: (*Voice over*) 'The doctor came again today. Dad looks ever so sad most of the time now. I told him that old joke of yours about Mrs Simpson the other day but I think he must have heard it before. You know how he usually laughs. He used to say I should go on the halls one day. Wish we could go to the Shepherd's Bush Empire again. Elsie and Doris Waters were on *Saturday Night Music-Hall*. And Stainless Stephen, and Oliver Wakefield. Mum says he's suggestive. Oh, and the Western Brothers. He used to take me every Saturday. Hope they don't bomb it . . .'

59. INT. KITCHEN. DAY

MOTHER, DOCTOR, SCHOOLS ATTENDANCE OFFICER and JOHN *seated in corner.*

JOHN: (*Voice over*) 'The doctor's nice. But he says Dad should go into the sanatorium because it's too much for Mum to cope with. I think Dad wants to go but she says no. Not for Christmas anyway. I was scared stiff when the attendance officer came. He said I'd got to go to school sometime. Don't see why. It's miles to walk, not that I mind that but it's a rotten hole and I don't like to leave Dad on his own with no one to talk to. Even when he can't talk. Anyway, the doctor spoke to him and said my nerves weren't up to it for the moment and the inspector said we'd see what happened in the New Year.'

60. EXT. CLIFF TOP. DAY
From his height above the long beach JOHN *watches a* COUPLE *walking together. He waves and shouts at them.*

61. EXT. BEACH. DAY
A GIRL *of about 20 looks up and smiles. With her is a* YOUNG MAN, *slightly older. She smiles at him and they both wave at the little figure on the upper cliff.*

62. EXT. BEACH. DAY
JOHN *runs towards the couple excitedly. The* GIRL *kisses him and the three of them walk by the sea together. She takes the* MAN's *arm and holds* JOHN's *hand.*

JOHN: (*Voice over*) 'I've made friends with a smashing girl. She's called Isabel. She's ever so nice. She's 21. She's got a boy friend called Raymond. They're engaged. He's not in the Army because he's in a reserved occupation. I don't know what he does. They're really *friendly*. I go out for walks with them every day pretty well . . .'

63. INT. KITCHEN PARLOUR. DAY
ISABEL'S MOTHER, ISABEL, RAYMOND, JOHN *and the* GRANDMOTHER (*seated on her own in the corner by the fire, dressed entirely in black, with overcoat, mittens and hat*) *are having tea.*

JOHN: (*Voice over*) 'Her mum runs a little hotel at St Lawrence called the Carfax. There's no one there at the moment. They say the Army's taking it over. Hope so. Her mum's nice too. They treat me like one of them. Except for the granny. She's a bit boring. Isabel says she hasn't had a bath for years. She certainly does *stink*. Phew! We had a smashing tea. Why do they all keep saying it will all be over by Christmas?'

ISABEL'S MOTHER: Well, that's what I think, anyway. What do you think, John. How long do you think it will last?

JOHN: (*Chewing thoughtfully*) Oh. Five years I should say.

ISABEL'S MOTHER: Would you? Well, I hope you're wrong.

JOHN: I don't.

ISABEL'S MOTHER: You wouldn't like Isabel to have to go and work in munitions would you?

JOHN: No, I jolly well wouldn't.

GRANDMA: (*Like a Giles cartoon*) That boy's got something wrong with him, he has.

ISABEL'S MOTHER: He's just got no one to talk to, that's all.

GRANDMA: He'll end up funny, you see.

RAYMOND: Well, he's quite funny now.

ISABEL: What does he call you?

RAYMOND: Professor Hugg.

(*They laugh.*)

GRANDMA: You'll see.

64. EXT. UPPER CLIFF. DAY

ISABEL *and* RAYMOND *are locked in an embrace on the ground.* JOHN *watches them.*

JOHN: (*Voice over*) 'I wish I could go and live with Isabel. And Raymond, I suppose. She's ever so nice. Really. They're always kissing and cuddling when we go on walks. For hours and hours. They don't seem to mind me being there ... If I was Raymond, I'd marry her straight away. *I* wouldn't wait.'

(*The* COUPLE *get up, adjusting themselves.* ISABEL *puts a hand out to* JOHN *and the three of them start walking.*)

65. EXT. SANATORIUM. DAY

The sanatorium, near Ventor. Long, gloomy Victorian building with rows of balconies for the patients to lie outside in the cold air. Beds, PATIENTS, NURSES.

66. EXT. SANATORIUM ENTRANCE. DAY

Two UNIFORMED MEN *lift John's* FATHER *from the ambulance in a wheelchair, watched by* JOHN *and his* MOTHER. *They follow the chair into the building.*

67. INT. SANATORIUM. DAY

The three of them wait in silence. Presently a NURSE *appears.*

NURSE: Mr Osborne? All ready for you.

(MOTHER *and* JOHN *go to follow him.*)

26

You can come, Mrs Osborne. But I should let the little boy
stay where he is.
(*They leave him seated in the corridor. From his pocket he takes
out the* Dandy *and three Penguin books:* Ariel, A Safety
Match *and* Death of a Hero)

68. INT. BEDROOM. DAY
*Close-up of a picture of a Finnish soldier, a white, hooded figure on
skis with a gun slung over his shoulder.* JOHN *is pinning it up beside
his map of Europe with its flags pinned all over it. He stands back
to look at it. His* MOTHER *is watching him, biting her nails
irritably. The wireless is playing* (Saturday Night Music-Hall
perhaps).

MOTHER: What's that, then?

JOHN: Finnish soldiers. You can't see them on the snow in
these suits. They're so fast the Russians don't know what's
hit them.

MOTHER: Bloody war. That's all you think about. Just wait till
you have to go. You won't be so bloody keen then. And
turn that wireless off! Gets on my nerves. All day. The
school inspector's right. Sooner you get off to school the
better. And you're not to keep bothering your father. You
go in when I tell you.

JOHN: I'll take his tea in.

MOTHER: I've done it. Doesn't want any.

JOHN: I'll see if he wants to read . . .

MOTHER: You heard what I said. He's not going to be here
much longer.

JOHN: What?

MOTHER: Oh, just listen, can't you? Didn't I say turn off that
bloody wireless! You have too much of that thing. (*Turns it
off.*) It's time you bucked up your ideas – instead of
mooning about with that Isabel and her young man. They
don't want *you* hanging about.

JOHN: Yes. They do. They told . . .

MOTHER: Well, you're to leave them alone. I've got no one to
talk to all day. Bloody dead-and-alive hole. All bloody
Isabel this and Isabel that, that and bloody war and

27

wireless. Try and think about somebody else for a change. You're *selfish*, that's what you are. You are, aren't you? Do you ever think what I'm going through?

(*Silence.*)

Your father's only got six weeks left.

JOHN: Six weeks . . .

MOTHER: You heard! Six weeks. That's what they said at the hospital. They wanted him in for Christmas but I wouldn't have it.

JOHN: Christmas?

MOTHER: I don't know what we're going to do. We should never have come here. Give me the bombs anytime to this bloody place. What's the matter with you?

(*His face is crumpled with silent tears.*)

Oh, don't *you* start bloody grizzling. I've got quite enough on my mind. Don't pretend you're surprised – you didn't think he could go on like this, did you? I must have a look at the copper if you're going to have a bath. I'll call you – no, you can go out and get the bath in. You're the one who left it in the garden.

(*She goes out, pauses.*)

(*Shouting up the stairs*) Dad! (*No reply. She goes downstairs. JOHN stands still, turns on the wireless ('Run rabbit, run' – Flanagan and Allen), picks up the three Penguin books, and slowly slumps on the bed, with them face down, trembling slightly.*)

69. EXT. UPPER CLIFF. DAY

JOHN *looks down to the undercliff at the solitary figure of* ISABEL *walking along the beach. (Music: 'Somewhere in France with you' – Vera Lynn.) He takes out his binoculars and watches her slow progress.*

70. INT. BEDROOM. NIGHT

JOHN *is in bed, half asleep. The door opens quietly and a dim figure is outlined in the door. Presently, the door is closed again. He is awake and puts the light on over his bed. On his orange-box desk beside him is a snapshot of Isabel, propped up against a model*

*Heinkel or Messerschmitt or whatever. He stares at it. Then he gets
out of bed and goes over to the corner of the room where there is a
half-full pillow case. He shivers, puts on his dressing-gown and
starts to empty the case. The parcels include things like games, ludo,
model tank, anti-aircraft gun with searchlight, highland soldiers
('Ladies from Hell') Boy's Own Annual for* 1940. *He opens it. The
inscription reads:* CHRISTMAS 1939. TO SKIPPER: LOVE DAD.
*He flips through the pages. There is also a Hurricane glider and,
best of all, a small model yacht. On the mast is a label with the
words written on it:* DON'T FORGET WHAT I TOLD YOU: THE
ROYAL NAVY ALWAYS TRAVELS FIRST CLASS. IT'S THE ONLY
WAY, DAD.

71. INT. KITCHEN. DAY
FATHER, MOTHER *and* JOHN *are seated for their Christmas
dinner.* FATHER, *thinner and paler than ever, with a heavy growth
of beard, looks almost like a very frail prophet, in his dressing-gown.
On the wireless, the King's Christmas speech.*
MOTHER: Try and eat it up, Dad.
FATHER: Just having half-time –
MOTHER: I made your bread sauce special. It's got real cream
    from next door. And the onion you like and the chilli –
FATHER: Yes. It'll be nice cold too.
MOTHER: Not like your mother's, I know.
FATHER: I told you – it's just right.
MOTHER: Well, drink up your Moussec. I thought you'd like
    that.
FATHER: The champagne of the poor.
MOTHER: It's wonderful the way the King does with that
    stammer. She must be a great help to him.
FATHER: I expect so.
MOTHER: *He* doesn't look very strong.
FATHER: Perhaps we should have another toast.
JOHN: How old are you, Dad?
FATHER: Dirty-nine.
JOHN: Cor, you'll be forty! (*Blushes and tries to cover up.*) I'll
    have to start saving up for your birthday.

29

FATHER: I shouldn't worry, son. It's not till May the 8th. It's a long time ahead. Give the boy a glass of port.

MOTHER: Do you think he should? He's had one – *and* a drop of my Guinness.

(FATHER *looks at her.*)

Oh, all right, it is Christmas. Here's to us then.

(*The other two don't drink.*)

FATHER: What about you then, son?

JOHN: They all said it would be over by Christmas.

FATHER: Perhaps it will be *next* Christmas ...

JOHN: Bet it won't.

FATHER: Well, I suppose we'd better toast the King. In the Navy, they always do it sitting down: The King!

(*They drink.*)

JOHN: And beating the Germans!

FATHER: (*Looking at his three sixpenny Penguins*) Thank you, son. I didn't mean you to buy *three*. Oh, well – one of them will do for my birthday.

MOTHER: Well, don't let's sit here getting morbid. If you're not going to eat that up, I'll go and get the pudding.

(*She goes out.*)

FATHER: (*Very quietly*) If that woman doesn't ... go soon ... I shall scream ...

(*She brings in the flaming pudding and turns out the light. The flames light up the faces of* JOHN *and his* FATHER *as she places it on the table.*)

72. EXT. BEACH. DAY

JOHN *sailing his yacht in a rock pool. Presently* ISABEL *and* RAYMOND *appear arm in arm. They don't see him. He watches them from behind the rocks.*

73. INT. BEDROOM/STAIRS. DAY

FATHER *in bed. He is reading* Ariel. *Then puts it down.* JOHN *is reading an illustrated article on sailing ships in the* Boy's Own Annual. *He watches his* FATHER *as he closes his eyes.*

FATHER: (*Muttering*) Out, keep her out ...

(JOHN *gets up and slips quietly out of the door, closing it behind*

30

him carefully. His MOTHER *is standing there. They say nothing as he passes her and goes downstairs to his room.*)

74. INT. BEDROOM. NIGHT

JOHN *is reading the* Boy's Own. *Isabel's photograph is now in a frame. Suddenly there is a scream. It is his* MOTHER. *He rushes to his door.*

75. INT. STAIRCASE. NIGHT

At the top of the stairs, his FATHER *is standing, completely naked, a white, powdery figure, illuminated only by the light from the candle he is holding. He stares sightlessly ahead of him. Then he puts one foot forward to descend the first step.* MOTHER *screams. He falters. The candle droops in his hand.*

MOTHER: Oh, my God! Do something! Oh, God. He's gone blind!

(*His* FATHER *sways and he falls head first at* JOHN's *feet.*)

76. EXT. UPPER CLIFF. DAY

Binocular view of ISABEL *clambering over rocks. The binoculars are lowered, revealing a* MAN *in his sixties.* JOHN *is watching him.*

JOHN: Can you see her, Grandad?

GRANDAD: Oh yes, they're good binoculars. German, yes . . . She's a very pretty woman. Engaged, is she?

JOHN: Yes. But they don't know when they're getting married. Because of the war. I wouldn't let it stop me.

(*They walk on.*)

GRANDAD: *You're* a bit young to be interested in girls.

JOHN: She's my friend. My best friend. She gave me a book on Nelson for Christmas.

GRANDAD: Well, you can't have too many friends, John. That's been your father's trouble. People never took to him much. Not even his own mother . . . least of all . . . How do you get on with *your* mum?

JOHN: Is it true the Royal Navy always travels first class?

GRANDAD: I suppose so, son. But it's not easy. It never is. And it's not going to be for you. Try not to forget that, boy. As you grow up. You have to learn how to mix.

JOHN: Mix.

31

GRANDAD: You can't sail the ship all on your own. Not unless you're very clever. Even then it's a hard business.
(*They walk on,* ISABEL's *figure receding on the beach below.*)

77. INT. BEDROOM. DAY
MOTHER *is leaning against the door.* GRANDFATHER *leads* JOHN *into the room. On the trestle is an open coffin.*
GRANDAD: (*Softly*) It's all right, boy.
(*He leads him over to the coffin.* JOHN *is just able to look down into it at his* FATHER. *After a while he turns and runs down to his room. The old man stares down at his son for a while, then moves over to* MOTHER. *She closes the door and locks it.*)
MOTHER: That room'll have to be fumigated.

78. INT. BEDROOM. NIGHT
MOTHER *is in* JOHN's *bed reading the* News of the World. *He winces as she rustles pages and turns to look at his photographs.*

79. EXT. HOUSE. DAY
Removal van with MEN *loading it with furniture.*

80. INT. EXT. BEDROOM/BEACH. DAY
JOHN *watching the beach from his window. He catches sight of* ISABEL *and runs down the stairs, past the* REMOVAL MEN *and his* MOTHER.
MOTHER: Here, where are you bloody gallivanting off to? We've got to catch that ferry.

81. EXT. CLIFF TOP. DAY
JOHN *runs frantically after the retreating figure of* ISABEL *on the beach below. He calls out, but the wind muffles his voice. He trips and falls. All he can see now is the clouds hovering over the sea.*

82. INT. CREMATORIUM. DAY
JOHN, *his* MOTHER *and* GRANDFATHER *stand as the voice of a* CLERGYMAN *reads the service. The coffin is resting on its plinth. There is a rattle of machinery as the coffin lurches on rails towards the purple curtain beyond. It disappears.* (*Music: 'A Life on the ocean wave'.*)

83. EXT. MICKEY'S HOUSE. DAY
*Sky. The Hurricane glider wheels and swoops against vast blue sky.
It plops to earth. Down to* JOHN *and* MICKEY *lying on the small
patch of suburban back garden. They are playing a game of
'flicking' cigarette cards.*

JOHN: Do you think we'll ever go back to Bognor again?

MICKEY: Don't know. (*looking at a card*) Here, that's a Len
    Hutton. Do you want it?

JOHN: You can have it.

MICKEY: There's a King's East African Rifles here you can
    have.

JOHN: Ta. Wonder if *we* could join the LDV. Don't see why
    not.

MICKEY: Dad says it's just a lot of drilling with sticks.
    Wouldn't mind the ARP.

JOHN: Or the Observer Corps.
    (*He picks up the cards. Siren sounds. They look up. They stand
    expectantly. Presently a black column of approaching planes
    appears like a flock of birds high in the bright blue sky. They
    turn and look behind them, enthralled.*)

84. EXT. SKY. DAY
*A similar flock appears from the opposite direction. Flashing silver
in the sun, flying directly towards the oncoming German planes.*

85. EXT. GARDEN. DAY
JOHN *and* MICKEY *look up. They have a grandstand view.*

86. FILM INSERT
The converging aircraft as from the viewpoint of JOHN *and*
MICKEY. *The Battle of Britain, or similar.*

87. EXT. GARDEN. DAY
*A girl of about 19 leans out of the top window of the house. It is
Mickey's sister,* EDNA.

EDNA: You silly little sods! Here! Didn't you hear the siren?
    (*Looks up.*) Oh, my God. What do you think you're doing?

33

MICKEY: Oh, shut up, big arse!
EDNA: You heard me. Can't you see them? Have you gone
   barmy, you two? Mickey! John! If you don't come in, I'll
   tell Dad.

88. FILM INSERT
*The two fleets approach each other. Suddenly they break this
implacable formation and the dogfight begins.*

89. EXT. GARDEN. DAY
The small figures of JOHN *and* MICKEY *in the garden staring
upwards. The noise is tremendous. Up to barrage balloon. Silent.
Down to . . .*

90. EXT. LONG SUBURBAN STREET. DAY
JOHN *and* MOTHER. *She is carrying a heavy suitcase, he another,
has gas-mask case bumping against him and another bag. He stops
to put them down for a moment.*
MOTHER: Oh, do stop dawdling. What's the matter with you?
JOHN: My arms ache.
MOTHER: So do mine and I'm not grizzling. It's that bloody
   rubbish you brought.
JOHN: It's my shrapnel –
MOTHER: I told you not to bring it. Come on, then. Here we
   are. Number 180.
   (*He staggers up with his load and follows her through the front
   gate of one of hundreds of drab semis stretching away to the
   London skyline. They go to the front door which is opened by a*
   WOMAN *in curlers and kitchen apron.*)
   Mrs Williams? We've come about the rooms.
   (MRS WILLIAMS *looks at them suspiciously and* JOHN *in
   particular.*)
   In the paper-shop window . . .
   (*She nods and they follow her into the house.*)

91. INT. HOUSE. DAY
Narrow hall, leading to kitchen.
MRS WILLIAMS: You'll have to tell me when you want to use

the kitchen. Twelve and six a week. In advance. Bath is one
and six. Fridays and Saturdays. Saturdays is best. I usually
go to my daughter-in-law's at the weekend. She's on her
own now my son's in the RAF.

MOTHER: Oh, we won't be any trouble.

MRS WILLIAMS: *I* hope not. He's a sergeant air-gunner.

MOTHER: Oh, nice. I'm out all day at Carter's seed factory.
Peace work. Then in the evenings I work part-time at the
Toby Jug.

MRS WILLIAMS: What about him?

MOTHER: Oh, he's ever so quiet. Head stuck in a book all the
time. It's all war with him. All he ever thinks about. Drives
you potty.

MRS WILLIAMS: Wait till it's *his* turn.

MOTHER: That's what I tell him. Won't think it's so funny
then. Anyway, he'll be at school all day. He'll take
sandwiches. Just up the road.

MRS WILLIAMS: Oh yes. Good at school, are you?

MOTHER: Can't get him to go. Just wants to sit at home all day.
Always got something wrong with him. Well, he'll have to
go now. He'll have the inspector after him now. Hasn't got
his dad to make excuses for him now. You'll *have* to go
now, won't you?

MRS WILLIAMS: What about if there's an air raid? If it gets
bad, I go to my daughter-in-law.

MOTHER: Oh, he's used to being on his own. He's not like me.
I can't stand it. I like a bit of company and a joke. Can't
stand sitting around getting morbid.

92. EXT. BACK GARDEN. DAY

MRS WILLIAMS *is showing them her Anderson shelter.*

MRS WILLIAMS: I never go in it unless it gets very bad. Can't
stand being shut in. Rather get killed.
(JOHN *pulls aside the curtains of the Anderson and peers in.*
There are four bare bunks, a candle, a teapot on a wooden box,
balls of knitting wool and an oil stove.)

MOTHER: Come out of there. You'll get damp on your chest.

93. INT. BEDROOM. DAY
Early light coming through cracks in black-out boards at windows.
JOHN *is asleep in bed, his pyjama jacket open, revealing his bony chest. Alarm clock goes off. He swings over the side of the bed, shivering, wincing as his bare feet touch the cold linoleum. He takes down the black-out boards at the window. A distant barrage balloon.*

94. EXT. STREET. DAY
JOHN *walking to school, with satchel and gas mask. He stops outside the playground of Chadacre Road Junior School. Within the gates is a pandemonium of* BOYS *and* GIRLS, *fighting etc. A sharp blast and whistle as a* WOMAN TEACHER *appears.* JOHN *joins the rows of* CHILDREN *as they line up to a series of shouts and whistles and then march into the school.*

95. INT. SCHOOL HALL. DAY
A whippy cane slashes down on to an outstretched hand. Several times.

96. INT. SCHOOL HALL. DAY
A SMALL BOY *tucks his hands beneath his armpits for comfort and joins half-a-dozen other* BOYS *on the rostrum where the* HEADMASTER *has been administering this in front of everyone in the school. Wearing a beret and looking like a particularly mean shop steward, he whacks the cane down on the table behind him.*
HEADMASTER: Now, if I hear of anyone else sneaking off home during an air raid, practice or not, that's what they'll get, only double. Any member of the staff will send them straight to me. Got it? Right. Dismiss!

97. INT. CLASSROOM. DAY
JOHN *is standing at a desk with another* BOY. *The class is singing* 'The Harp that Once'.
BOY: (*Singing*) '. . . that once through Tara's balls . . .' Bet we go down the shelters. Better than arithmetic.
TEACHER: All right. Gas masks! Drill! Come on. Get on with it then.

36

(*The* CLASS *do their drill. Giggling noisily. The* BOY *amuses himself making farting noises when he's got his gas mask on, miming some primitive.*)

BOY: (*Shouting, muffled*) Wallah wallah oompa! Wallah wallah oompa.

(JOHN *struggles into his.*)

98. INT. CLASSROOM. DAY
From JOHN's *point of view, within the gask mask. The eye-piece is steaming from his breath and the blurred, cloudy figures of the* CHILDREN *in the classroom, the* TEACHER *and the deafening noise and the* BOY *jeering his 'Wallah wallah oompa' at him become nightmarish. An air-raid siren sounds, whistles blow, increased uproar. He tears off the mask, frightened and gasping.*

99. INT. SCHOOL CORRIDOR. DAY
JOHN *joins the yelling file of* CHILDREN *as they are dragooned by a warder-like* TEACHER *off to the shelter.*

100. EXT. PLAYGROUND. DAY
Shelter in sportsfield. The CHILDREN *are piling into the long above-ground brick shelter.* JOHN *looks around for a way to escape. As he is about to run, a* TEACHER *blocks his path.*

TEACHER: Where do you think you're going?

JOHN: Lavatory, sir.

TEACHER: Don't be bloody stupid. It's not a picnic. Now get in there. Go on, get in or I'll send you to the headmaster. Get a move on!

(*He punches him fiercely in the back.* JOHN *gasps with pain and staggers in to the screaming black pit of the shelter.*)

101. INT. SHELTER. DAY
Shouting, whistling. JOHN *finds himself squashed on to the end of the bench. A dark, dripping hole crammed with yelling, balaclavaed, stinking, mostly dirty* CHILDREN. *Fists, boots on shins in a black uproar. The* TEACHER *moves down the line, hitting* CHILDREN *on all sides, shouting at them. They subside a little at this indiscriminate savagery and start singing/shouting.*)

37

CHILDREN: (*Singing*) There was rats, rats,
>Big as blooming cats,
>In the stores,
>In the Quartermaster's stores.

(*Frenzy.*)
>My eyes are dim I cannot see.
>I have not brought my specs with me.
>I have no—ot brought my—y specs with me.

(*And so it goes on hysterically.* JOHN *is bashed heartily on the arm because he isn't singing. Someone kicks his legs repeatedly. No way of defence. He looks round for the* TEACHER *to turn his back. When he does so, he hurls himself through the open entrance.*)

VOICE: (*Calling*) Hey, you! you can't do that. You won't half get it.

(*The* TEACHER *turns.*)

TEACHER: Shut up! I'll send you *all* up after.

BOY: Mr Blundell, sir! He's gone. He went out.

TEACHER: Who did?

BOY: Don't know. That twot sitting next to me.

TEACHER: Shut up or *you'll* get it. Keep bloody singing if you've got to.

(They howl 'Roll out the barrel'.)

102. EXT. PLAYGROUND/STREETS. DAY

JOHN, *trailing his gas-mask case, crashes into the boys' lavatory. He slides behind the door, panting. 'Roll out the Barrel' is coming over loud and clear. The* TEACHER'S *head looks out from the shelter. Seeing nothing, he goes back inside.* JOHN, *like an escaping POW, suddenly makes a dash across the empty playground. Through the Gates, he runs as fast as he can. His cap falls off as he goes down the deserted street. A low-flying fighter aircraft suddenly zooms behind him. He throws himself down on the muddy verge. It screams past him. Machine-gun sounds. He lies in the icy mud. It is still again. He gets up and goes into the back yard of a house and crouches by a coal bunker. A cat, sitting inside on the coal, stares at him. He crouches. Waiting.*

103. EXT. COAL BUNKER. DAY

A WOMAN *comes out of the back door.*

WOMAN: Here, what you think *you're* doing?
  (*The all-clear sounds. They stare at each other.*)
  You're not supposed to be here. You should be in the
  shelter. I know. My boy's at your school.
  (*He races off back to the street.*)
  I'll report you. You'll get the cane you will!

104. EXT. PLAYGROUND. DAY

JOHN *is running to catch up with the other* BOYS *and* GIRLS *who
are trooping into the school. Hiding behind a wall, he looks for an
opportunity to join them unnoticed. Suddenly a large hand grabs his
ear. It is the* TEACHER.

TEACHER: (*Twisting his ear*) Where do you think you've been?
JOHN: Lavatory, sir. *Ow!*
TEACHER: The Germans don't like little boys going to the
  lavatory when they're dropping their great big bombs.
  Now, don't let me catch you again. Now, hop it!
JOHN: Thank you, sir.
  (*He runs off.*)

105. EXT. GARDEN. NIGHT

In dressing-gown and pyjamas JOHN *makes his way into the
Anderson shelter. He flashes his torch inside and goes in.*

106. INT. ANDERSON SHELTER. NIGHT

Dark. JOHN *strikes a match and lights a candle on his box table. He
looks around him. On the damp aluminium walls are identification
posters of enemy aircraft: The Heinkel, Dornier, Messerschmitt, etc.
Beside him is a thermos flask and sandwiches. He looks out into the
night sky, then clambers into bed, covered with woollies, balaclava,
mittens and so on. He settles down comfortably to read. His*
MOTHER *puts her head in.*

MOTHER: All right then, are you?
JOHN: Yes, thank you.
MOTHER: Thank you, *what?* Mummy? What is it? Too big to
  bring yourself to say it? Well. Well, I'm off down the pub

39

now before the siren goes. That warden at number 93 waits for me coming. Look, you'll be all right without Mrs Williams, won't you?

JOHN: (*Can't wait for her to go.*) Fine.

MOTHER: Where's me torch...? I expect I'll be stuck under that bloody billiard table again all night if it goes on. You're sure you'll be all right?

JOHN: (*Reading*) Sure.

MOTHER: Well, you're a cool one. Head in a book all night suits you just right, doesn't it? Perhaps you won't make such a bad sailor after all. Well, try and get some sleep, I can't have you being ill again. Can't stand any more bloody illness in my life. I've had my share. I'd go mad in here. You're a funny kid. Isn't half damp in here. You'll get pneumonia, if it's not a bomb. Well, I'm off for a bit of *life*. Bye...

(*She disappears.* JOHN, *relieved, snuggles down to his books and comics. The siren sounds. Then all is quiet.*)

VOICE: (*Shouting*) Put that light out. *You* – stop flashing that bloody torch!

(JOHN *grins. It grows still. Then the sound of anti-aircraft fire. Presently the relentless, low buzz of approaching bombers. He goes back to his reading. The sound of the bombers comes closer. He looks up, gets out of his bunk, draws the curtains and looks up at the sky, streaked with searchlights. A shrill whistling sound. The tiny shelter shakes. He throws himself into his bunk. A bomb has exploded. He waits. Another. The candle is blown out from the flapping curtain. Blackness. A match is struck and he relights the candle, listens. Whistles, shake, explosion, even nearer. His books fall to the floor, the flask is upset, his mug breaks and posters fall off the walls. The hum of the aircraft continues. After a while he picks up his annual and reads. It is going to be a long night.*)

107. INT. ANDERSON SHELTER. DAY

Early daylight slides through the curtain. JOHN *is asleep. The all-clear sounds. He doesn't wake. His* MOTHER's *face peers in.*

MOTHER: Thank God, you're all right! I couldn't wait for the

all-clear. That policeman stopped me again. 'Look,' I said,
'it's no use your stopping me, my little boy's at home all on
his own. Besides I've got to be on shift at eight o'clock.'
(*He blinks at her.*)
Still bloody reading, I suppose. I don't know. Sometimes I
think you can't have any feelings at all. Like a bloody
German yourself, you are. Well, come on, then. I got some
eggs off Eric's barrow. Didn't half cost me too. Don't know
what I'd do without tips. You'll be late for school again.
Number 93 got it. And next door at Chadacre Road. Go on
– shift yourself!

108. EXT. STREET. DAY
JOHN *comes out of the house with gas mask and packet of
sandwiches, etc. He gets to the gate and pauses to look at number 93.
He runs across the street to watch* FIREMEN *picking among the
rubble of the completely demolished house.*

109. EXT. STREET. DAY
Street on the way to the school. JOHN *walks on, watching a similar
scene. The street is crowded with people, ambulances, glass, debris.
People watch in groups.*

110. INT. SCHOOLROOM. DAY
A cane lashes down on to a small hand. Camera pulls back to reveal
HEADMASTER, *smoking a pipe and stepping back for another hefty
swipe. He puts down the cane on his carpentry bench.*
HEADMASTER: You know what they say: business as usual.
    Can't have boys being late. Wait till you get in the Army.
JOHN: (*Mumbling*) Navy –
HEADMASTER: Army, Navy, doesn't matter. You'll get shot
    for less than that. Don't you know there's a war on?
JOHN: Yes, sir.
HEADMASTER: What's your name?
JOHN: Osborne, sir.
HEADMASTER: Well, buck your ideas up, Osborne. We've all
    got to pull together. Can't have slackers in wartime. *Any*
    time. Don't let me see you again.

41

JOHN: No, sir.

HEADMASTER: Oh, just a minute. Here. (*Takes out a coin.*) Get
   me some tobacco on the corner. Say it's for me.

III. EXT. PLAYGROUND/STREET. DAY

JOHN, *locking his palms and tucking them beneath his armpits. The
air-raid siren sounds. He makes a dash for the freedom of the street,
released from the torment of the shelter. He runs down the street,
looks back to see the other* CHILDREN *trooping to safety. He grins as
he runs.*

II2. EXT/INT. STREET/SHOP. DAY

Tobacconist's and newsagent's shop. JOHN *opens the door and goes
inside. Aircraft sounds, gunfire. He looks around him. The shop is
empty. It starts to shake as a bomb drops. He dives to the floor.
Explosion. Dust rises from the shop and some of the stock falls to the
floor. Sweet jars, newspapers. He gets up slowly as it settles back
into quietness, looking to the back of the shop. The head of the*
NEWSAGENT *appears from above the counter. He looks astonished
to see the boy.*

JOHN: The headmaster wants some of his tobacco. Two ounces.

NEWSAGENT: Blimey!

   (*Shakily, he weighs out some shag on to a pair of scales.*)

II3. INT. CUPBOARD BENEATH STAIRS. NIGHT

Sitting in the light of a candle between them, JOHN *and his*
MOTHER *are crouched, barely able to sit up straight.* MOTHER *is
dressed with an overcoat over her clothes. She wears curlers as she
reads the* Mirror, *smoking furiously, biting her nails as she glares
across clouds of smoke at her son. He is listening to the radio:*
Saturday Night Music-Hall, Garrison Theatre, Itma, *or
something of the kind.*

MOTHER: My day off and all. They would, wouldn't they?
   Anyway, I'm not going down that damp hole out there.
   You look dreadful. If you ask me, your dad's the lucky one.
   He's in the right place. Got a bit of peace, anyway. That's
   where we'll all be soon. Well, don't just sit there – say
   something to your mother. Listen! They're coming over
   again! Listen! Turn that bloody thing off! I can't hear . . .

42

(*He does so. They listen. The cupboard shudders at a distant explosion. Light flickers. The aircraft pass and it is still again.*) Seems quiet for a minute. Here, go and get me that half-bottle of gin Eric give me. No, I suppose *I'd* better get it. You'll only say you can't find it. I want to *go* anyway. Sh! (*Listens.*) Do you think it'll be quiet for a bit?

JOHN: They'll be back soon.

MOTHER: Oh – cheerful!

JOHN: They always do.

MOTHER: Mister Bloody Know-all, that's what they call you at school. Well – I'm going to risk it. I'm bursting. Don't *you* want to go?

JOHN: No, thanks.

(*She hesitates.*)

MOTHER: Well, I'm off then.

(*She squeezes out and dashes to the kitchen, then upstairs. He waits. Aircraft suddenly start pounding. Hum of bombers. A deafening swishing sound, the cupboard seems to move in anticipation before the bomb falls. The whole house shudders just before the impact.*)

114. INT. HALLWAY. NIGHT

The bomb explodes. The black-out boards disappear as the windows are blown out. The street door is lifted out into the garden. The ceiling falls in. JOHN *emerges after a while. Plaster and dust cover him. From upstairs is a scream and sounds of wailing. He goes to the foot of the stairs and looks up. His* MOTHER *appears, a grey, curlered apparition, clutching a shattered gin bottle, her knickers around her ankles. She stumbles down the stairs, clutching at the broken banister, moaning. She gets to within a stair or so of her son, her face streaming with grime, panic and rage. He stares at her. They gaze at each other in silence as the mess settles.* JOHN *breaks into uncontrollable, happy laughter. She watches him in fury as he goes on.*

MOTHER: (*Screaming*) Shut up! I said shut up!

(*He can't – and won't – stop. She swings the back of her hand across his face, stopping him for a moment. But giggles overcome him again.*)

115. INT. CINEMA. EVENING
Newsreel. Bombed street. Scenes similar to what JOHN *had seen only much worse.* JOHN *and* MICKEY *watch. Then scenes of destroyers escorting convoys, George Formby entertaining troops, etc. Lights come up. Cinema organ appears from the pit. Selection: 'Sergeant major on parade', 'I do like to be beside the seaside', etc.*

116. EXT. CINEMA. EVENING
JOHN *and* MICKEY *coming out.*

JOHN: My grandmother had to walk all the way from Fulham to
     Bond Street Woolworths . . . Had no gas for weeks. Bet we
     get no Christmas dinner.
MICKEY: At least they can't say it'll all be over by Christmas
     this time.
JOHN: You bet. It's just started. That's what I told Mum. She
     wasn't half mad.
     (*They laugh and run off into the dark.*)
     Here, where's your torch – I can't bloody well see . . .

117. INT. KITCHEN/DINING ROOM. NIGHT
Shabby. Very Victorian. Candlelight. GRANDAD *is listening to the King's speech.* MOTHER *is smoking and looking aimless as she drinks her gin.* GRANDAD *looks solemn, reading the* News of the World *as he listens. He's rather dapper in an Edwardian way, smoking a cigarette through a holder.* GRANDMA *is cooking a chicken over a candle in a bucket. She's the only one who looks cheerful.* JOHN *watches her.*

GRANDMA: What did you friend Mick give you for Christmas
     then?
JOHN: A book. It's called the *Black-out Book.* It's 101 things to
     do in the black-out.
GRANDMA: Oh, yes? Don't give it to your grandfather then.
     Have another drop of port.
MOTHER: You're not giving him any more of that port are you,
     Mum? You know what he's like. He'll only be sick all the
     way home like last time.

GRANDMA: Oh, it's Christmas. Won't do him any harm.

MOTHER: And don't get Queenie on to religion after dinner, either. You know what she's like. I don't want any more rows. I've had enough in my life. If it's not bloody religion it's money. God and money, that's all she ever thinks about. Bloody morbid.

GRANDAD: Hold your bloody noise, will you? I'm trying to listen. And put the wood in the 'ole, will you? You weren't born in a field, were you? (*To* JOHN, *who is closing the door*) I don't know about *you*.
(*National anthem.*)
There I've missed the end. Well, go on all of you, stand up! Where are your glasses? I don't know.
(*They all stand.*)

JOHN: They toast the King sitting down in the Royal Navy.

GRANDAD: Well, you're not in the Royal bloody Navy – *yet*!

MOTHER: I don't know where he gets them damn silly ideas. The sooner Dad's Society sends him away to boarding school the better. They'll soon knock it out of him.

GRANDAD: Hold your noise! The King!

ALL: The King!
(GRANDAD *looks across at the chicken his wife is holding over the bucket.*)

GRANDAD: And as for you, you want your head examined.

GRANDMA: Nearly ready. (*Winks at* JOHN) Come on, let's look at the potatoes. Don't know what you can do if you don't try.
(JOHN *follows her into the scullery where a saucepan containing sprouts and potatoes is simmering on an ancient oil stove.*)

GRANDAD: (*From the* News of the World) There's some fellow here assaulted some poor woman, committed bigamy and – what – yes, supposed to have raped his first wife.

GRANDMA: (*Grinning at* JOHN) *She's* the lucky one.

GRANDAD : What's that?

GRANDMA: Nearly done.

GRANDAD: Filthy beast. Should be locked away. Castrated.

GRANDMA: (*Softly*) Dirty old devil – he's worse than anyone. He had *two* women in here last week. And he's 72! While I was at work, coming back through the bombs. They got the convent last week. Land mine killed 103 nuns.

GRANDAD: Only 38. Why isn't he in the Army?

GRANDMA: Hand me that bucket over. Careful – it's hot.
(*He does so.*)
I had to chuck out Marie Lloyd from the bar when we were running the Duncannon. 'Don't you talk to me,' she said. 'I've just left your old man in an hotel in Brighton so you can something off!' she said. She had a filthy tongue. Still, he was different then. Smartest publican in London, they called him.

118. INT. KITCHEN/DINING ROOM. DAY

GRANDMA *brings in the chicken.* GRANDAD *starts to carve.*

MOTHER: Look at that, John. Isn't your Grandma clever? You may not get *this* next Christmas.

GRANDAD: Course he will. Pass your plate, Dolly . . .
Dardenelles, I was in the Dardanelles when I was 40. *That* was a fine mess. Back door to Europe they called it.

MOTHER: (*To* JOHN) You will eat it up, won't you? Don't you think he's looking a bit peaky? I put it down to that shelter. He lives in it. Damp and bloody miserable. He doesn't seem to mind at all. Oh, well, Happy Christmas everybody!

119. INT. BEDROOM. DAY

JOHN *is sitting up in bed, surrounded by books, his radio beside him. Mozart. He looks up as his* MOTHER *comes in, putting on her overcoat and snood.* MICKEY *following her*

MOTHER: Here's Mickey come to see you. (*To* MICKEY) Don't stay too long. He just gets overtired. And his temperature goes up. Did you take it at teatime? (*He nods.*)
What was it?

JOHN: 101.

MOTHER: Oh, blimey. Eight months we've had of this!

JOHN: It always goes up in the evening.

MOTHER: Eight months in bloody bed. He won't listen to me. Waited on hand and foot. You won't like it in a convalescent home. I'll be late for work. It's a Masonic do so I should make a bit tonight. Old Eric's getting some clothing coupons so I'll be able to pay for them. I'll be back late so don't sit there reading all night. (*To* MICKEY) Remember, *you*, off – early. And don't keep playing that bloody wireless all night. Mrs Williams gets upset and *I* have to carry the can. (*On the way out*) Oh, and don't try having a bath. You know what happened the last time. Anyway, we can't afford it. Just wait till Friday when I have mine. Where's my torch? Don't forget what I said, both of you.

MICKEY: G'night.

(*She goes.* JOHN *makes a face.*)

JOHN: I told her I'd go into hospital but she won't let me. Wouldn't have anyone to shout at, I suppose.

MICKEY: What *is* rheumatic fever?

JOHN: Don't know. Something to do with your heart. Doesn't half bang sometimes. Feel it.

(*He opens his pyjama jacket and* MICKEY *feels.*)

MICKEY: Cor. Is it always like that?

JOHN: No. When *she's* here it is. What you got there?

MICKEY: *Hotspur*, and *Rover* and the *Gem*.

JOHN: Don't like the *Rover*. What's 'Köchel' mean?

MICKEY: We had that in Music Appreciation. It's the name of some German bloke who made a list of everything Mozart ever wrote.

JOHN: Why do they say 'Vorshak' instead of 'De-vorak'?

MICKEY: Don't know. Might be in here.

JOHN: What's that?

(MICKEY *produces a large volume.*)

After all you say 'Ann Devorak' *not* 'Vorshak'.

MICKEY: *The Loom of Language* by Jespersens – or is it Hogben? It's philology.

JOHN: What's that?

MICKEY: Science of language.

JOHN: Blimey – wish I was clever. 'She' says Dad's society's going to send me to boarding school after the convalescent place. Hey. It's *Hi-Gang*.

(*He switches programmes.*)

RADIO: *Hi-Gang* coming to you from the heart of London . . .

Wish I could get a scholarship to your school. But mine won't be anywhere near. Somewhere stuck in the country, miles from anything, the war, everything.
(*They listen to* Hi-Gang. *A voice shouts up the stairs. It's the landlady.*)

MRS BARRATT: (*Out of vision*) Turn that flaming wireless off! You've had it on all day. Haven't you got any consideration for other people? (*Pause.*) If you don't turn it off, I'll tell your mother. You're a very selfish boy. You're not the only one, you know. Lucky you're not like my old man out in the desert with all the flies and things.
(*Doors slams.* JOHN *turns the radio right down and they both put their ears to it.*)

120. EXT. RAILWAY BRIDGE OVER STATION PLATFORMS. DAY

A train is moving out below JOHN *and his* MOTHER. *A* WOMAN *in blue raincoat, nurse's uniform approaches them. She wears pebble spectacles which make her look rather fearsome.*

NURSE: You're late.

MOTHER: We couldn't get a seat. Full of troops.

NURSE: That's him, is it, then?

MOTHER: Yes. You'll find he's very quiet. He's a good boy.

NURSE: (*Taking his small suitcase*) He'd better be. No excuses for boys even if they are sick. So are the poor soldiers. You should see some of the sights *I've* seen. Come on, then. Look smart.
(*She takes his hand briskly.*)

121. EXT. COUNTRY ROAD. DAY

Crocodile of SMALL BOYS *trooping along the empty road. They are singing 'Roll out the Barrel'. The* NURSE *leading them. She shouts at* JOHN, *who is trailing at the back.*

NURSE: Come on, you. Look alive! *If* you can.
(JOHN, *panting for breath, tries to catch up.*)

122. EXT. FOOTBALL FIELD. DAY

JOHN, *playing with* BOYS *mostly bigger than himself, the* NURSE *acting as referee, hectoring him for slowness.*

JOHN: (*Voice over*) 'This is a rotten place, the food's rotten and the nurses are rotten. It's like one of those Stalag places. I'm going to try and post this in the village. The lessons are stupid, we keep going for walks and then I have to lie down all the afternoon in the dormitory. There's only one other boy. He never says anything. He's like an old man. Nurse Atkins says he's got heart disease and he's going to die in six weeks. I had a fight with a boy the second day here. He was much bigger than me. He called me a twot. I didn't know what it meant but there didn't seem much else for it. Anyway, they sent me to the doctor and he said I'd have to stay here another six weeks as I'd damaged the valves of my heart. The matron was at Dartmouth College. She said if I'd been there I'd have been beaten without mercy.'

123. INT. LARGE VICTORIAN BARE ROOM. EVENING
MATRON, BOYS and a CLERGYMAN *preparing to give out presents. They are singing 'Star of Wonder'. MATRON looks grim.*
JOHN: (*Voice over*) 'Some of the boys are planning to escape but I didn't see the point. They only catch you. Three kids got as far as Hemel Hempstead but the police brought them back. They all look so old – and thin. Kids who wet the bed have to stand with their sheets over their heads while we have breakfast. They're starved already anyway. Boarding school can't be worse than *this*. What a way to spend Christmas . . .'

124. EXT. WATERLOO STATION. DAY
Crowded, SERVICEMEN *mostly. Loudspeaker plays popular wartime and martial music. Beside a waiting train* JOHN *stands waiting with his* MOTHER. *Other* BOYS *in grey flannel suits and their* PARENTS. *Corridor packed with* SOLDIERS, SAILORS.
MOTHER: Try and be a good boy. It's costing a lot of money you know. Work hard for God's sake – or I'll get it. Try and think of your father . . .
(*Whistle blows. He gets in and slams the door.*)
I'll get some sweet coupons from Eric and send them to you.

(*Doors slam. Guard's whistle.*)
Just think how lucky you are. There's no war down there.
You're out of it. Some of us have just got to get on with it.
Give us a kiss then.
(*He does so as perfunctorily as possible as the train moves out.*)

125. INT. RAILWAY CARRIAGE. DAY
JOHN *sits surrounded by noisy* BOYS, *thumping each other and
laughing. He looks out at the countryside. Then up at the face of a*
SAILOR *drinking a bottle of beer. The* SAILOR *winks and offers him
a swig.*
JOHN: Gosh, thanks!
(*Everyone sings 'Bless 'em all'.*)

126. INT. DORMITORY. DAY
*Close-up of Father's photograph being pinned to the wall. Draw
back to reveal* JOHN *looking at the photograph. About a dozen other*
BOYS *are unpacking and spreading things on their beds. A boy*
(WATSON) *approaches.*
WATSON: Your dad?
JOHN: Yes.
WATSON: Thin, isn't he? My dad played for London Welsh
    before the war. I'm Watson.
JOHN: Osborne.
    (*They shake hands.*)
BOY: (*Singing*) South of the border down Germany way,
        There's a little man I'd like to drown this very day,
        He should have been drowned the day of his birth,
        Old Schikelgruber, down Germany way.
WATSON: (*Seeing* JOHN's *ukelele*) Can you play that?
JOHN: Not really. Me mum got it off Eric's stall. I think I can
    play *one*.
WATSON: Go on, then. Shut up, you lot! Osborne's going to
    give a recital on his ukelele.
VOICE: 'With his little ukelele in his hand.'
    (*With sheets of music* JOHN *struggles through a few bars of
    'Don't fence me in'. They join in. A* PREFECT *appears at the
    door.*)

PREFECT: Here, *you*, George Formby – put that stupid thing away. What's your name?

JOHN: Osborne, sir.

PREFECT: Musical instruments are for the music room, not the dormitory. And don't call me 'sir'. Now, get downstairs, the lot of you.

(*They all rush.* JOHN *just saves his ukelele.*)

127. INT. SCHOOL HALL. EVENING

The HEADMASTER *is addressing the school.* JOHN *is standing beside* WATSON.

HEADMASTER: ... we have all got to make more and more effort. We must have no slacking either in class or out of it. Never forget the great sacrifices your parents are making for you, not only to keep you here but to see to it that we win through and, with God's help, right finally prevails. And not only your parents but people in all walks of life. There is no room for *slackness*. It is my unhappy task in greeting you back to announce sad news about some old boys. Eric Fisher, Major Fisher, who some of you may remember has been overseas for two years, in North Africa and Italy, and has received very serious arm and leg wounds in the Battle of the Gothic Line. Ironically, the hospital in which he is said to be recovering, facing the Isle of Capri, was once Mussolini's home. K. B. Symonds had a very bad motor-cycle accident in Africa and has been invalided out of the Dorset Regiment. Captain N. Munday is now in Italy with the famous comedian, Stainless Stephen. B. G. Merchant, who became a glider pilot, was killed in action in August. A full bulletin will be posted later. And now let us join in Arthur Clough's beautiful hymn: 'Say not the struggle nought availeth'.

(*They all sing.*)

128. INT. SCHOOLROOM. DAY

Close-up of pin-up of Lana Turner handed from desk to desk.
MASTER *in a clerical collar addresses the class. The pin-up reaches*

JOHN's *desk. He stares at it.*
JOHN: (*Whispering*) That's mine.
WATSON: (*In desk behind him*) I know. Banana Turner!
(*Grins all round.* JOHN *puts it in his desk surreptitiously, then looks out of the window. Across the sunny fields. A* GIRL *passes swinging a tennis racket. He watches her, fascinated.*)
JOHN: (*To* WATSON, *in whisper*) Who's that?
WATSON: Head's niece. No chance there.
(JOHN *goes on staring at her.*)

129. EXT. PLAYING FIELD. DAY
The HEAD'S NIECE *walking.*
JOHN: (*Out of vision*) What's her name?
WATSON: (*Out of vision*) Jenny. We've all tried. No oats there, mate.

130. INT. CLASSROOM. DAY
JOHN *is still staring out of the window.*
MASTER: (*Quietly*) Osborne . . .
(*He doesn't hear.*)
Osborne!
(JOHN *is startled.*)
How did John the Baptist die?
WATSON: (*In his ear*) Shot himself.
JOHN: Shot himself, sir.
(*Laughter.*)
MASTER: I see. Would you care to show us what you have just put into your desk?
(JOHN *takes out the photograph of Lana Turner and takes it up to him.*)
I see. You seem to have your priorities in life a little upside-down. I have noticed increasingly ever since you first came. You will see me afterwards.
JOHN: Sir.

131. INT. CLASSROOM. DAY
JOHN *on his own, writing.*
JOHN: (*Voice over*) 'Watson's not so bad, though he got me right

52

in it the other day. We spend hours feeding pigs and hoeing and potato-picking. I seem to be very behind in everything. I don't understand the questions, let alone the answers. Old Freddie says I may never catch up. That girl, Jenny, spoke to me on the way to chapel. She asked me if my name was Osborne. I couldn't think *why*. That's all she said. She made me think of Isabel. Grub gets worse and they keep telling us how lucky we are and about the North Atlantic convoys. We're being allowed to see a film called *Western Approaches* on Friday because it shows what the sailors have to put up with.'

132. FILM INSERT
Clip from Western Approaches. *Men in lifeboat. Surging seas.*

133. EXT. TENNIS COURT. DAY
JENNY *is playing another* GIRL. JOHN *and* WATSON *watch. From a classroom a sketchy attempt on the piano of 'Für Elise'.*
WATSON: Don't fancy all that being in a tiny boat, being frozen and covered with oil and stuff. Give me the RAF. Look – you can see her knickers.
JOHN: Shut up!
WATSON: You can. Look. Now! See? Green. (*Shouting*) Green!
    (JENNY *looks embarrassed and pulls at her skirt.*)
    Well, come on, you've got to do my English essay. Come on. She'll be wearing 'em tomorrow.
    (*Reluctantly*, JOHN *follows him.*)
JOHN: You *will* do my algebra, won't you?
WATSON: Sure. They know anyway.
JOHN: I'll never understand it. Don't want to either.
WATSON: You're not going a bit ga-ga on her are you?
JOHN: Course not.
WATSON: No joy there, I tell you. No joy.

134. EXT. COUNTRY LANE. DAY
JOHN *walks hand in hand with* JENNY.
JOHN: (*Voice over*) 'We didn't talk much. Just about school and things. And the war. She's not too interested in that, I don't think. But she listened.'

135. INT. SCHOOL HALL. DAY

HEADMASTER *addressing school.*

HEADMASTER: ... reminding me of that old verse:

> The sergeant met me by the road,
> Said he, 'My lad to me
> The war's begun, and now's the time
> For lads of six foot three.'

Finally, I must come to a very grave matter. A most distasteful one but as I know full well that you must be aware of it, either from the newspapers or gossip. For this reason, I asked the junior boys to leave. You will, as I say, have heard of the criminal proceedings taken against the Reverend Pearce. There were, I am thankful to say, no boys from this school involved ... but I feel I cannot possibly leave the matter without passing some comment on it ...

JOHN: What's this then?

WATSON: (*Grinning*) Poor old Pearce.

JOHN: (*Whispering*) What about him?

WATSON: Buggery. Caught with three sea scouts from Barnstaple.

JOHN: Blimey!

WATSON: Old Juicy had better watch it.

JOHN: What?

WATSON: Juicy Lemon. In old Freddie's room in the evenings.

JOHN: What do you mean? Why do they call him 'Juicy Lemon'?

WATSON: Search me. He's watching you.

(*They fall silent.*)

HEADMASTER: ... although I naturally don't feel it necessary to worry any boy at this school, with its healthy tradition of sporting, Christian manliness and high endeavour.

136. EXT. COUNTRY LANE. DAY

JOHN *and* WATSON *fooling about.*

BOTH: (*Singing*) The stars at night

Are big and bright
Deep in the heart of Texas.
(*Clap. Clap. Laughter.*)
WATSON: Hey, look. No, stop it. Look.
(*They stop. On the hedgerow is a long, slimy object, glistening almost like a spider's web with frost on it. It is a used french letter.*)
Bloody Yanks! That's the *third* one!
(*They stare.*)

137. EXT. FIELD. DAY
JOHN *and* JENNY *are lying on the grass locked in a kiss. Some fumbling.*
JENNY: No – be careful.
JOHN: All right. I've got an idea for next Sunday.
(*He kisses her.*)

138. EXT. MARKET TOWN STREET. DAY
Outside barber's. Durex ad in the window. Or, rather, just the word. JOHN *and* WATSON *arguing.*
JOHN: *You* go in this time.
WATSON: No, they know me now. Anyway, it's for you – not me.
JOHN: It was for you last time.
WATSON: Yes. And what happened? She went back to London. I gave 'em to Bowles for five bob. Three and six profit.
JOHN: You selfish bastard.
WATSON: *You* didn't have the three and six.
JOHN: Fuckpig! I've *got* to.
(*He looks around desperately.*)
WATSON: Well, go in, then! We'll miss the news.
(*An* AMERICAN SAILOR *is looking in the window of an antique shop next door.* JOHN *approaches him.*)
JOHN: Excuse me, sir.
SAILOR: Yeah?
JOHN: Er, I wonder if you would be so good as to help me, sir, do me a favour, sir?
SAILOR: Sure, kid. What is it?

JOHN: Well, it's rather a delicate matter, sir.
(*He looks around and takes the* SAILOR *by the arm to the shop doorway, and says something to him. The* SAILOR *whistles.*)
SAILOR: They usually ask for gum.
(*He puts his hand in his pocket and hands* JOHN *a tiny packet.*)
Help yourself. Compliments of Uncle Sam.
JOHN: Gosh!
(*The* SAILOR *smiles down at him.*)

139. EXT. FIELD. DAY

Over looking the estuary. SAILOR, JOHN *and* WATSON *sitting.*

SAILOR: The Navy's OK. They look after you. But I'd give it a miss if you can.
JOHN: Do you think we'll invade soon?
SAILOR: No idea.
WATSON: (*Pointing*) Are they *your* landing craft?
SAILOR: That's ours.
JOHN: They say two of your marines were killed on the beach at Salcombe on Wednesday.
SAILOR: Couldn't say about that . . . You look kind of desperate.
JOHN: Oh, it won't last much longer. Not even with the Yanks. Sorry, I mean.
SAILOR: No, I mean you're in a kind of a hurry, aren't you – generally? Not in love, are you?
JOHN: Well – I've got a girl . . . She's called Jenny.
SAILOR: (*Getting up*) Well, try not to upset Jenny too much. You seem a thoughtful kind of a kid. And don't think about the war too much. Have a ball while you can. Just see no one gets hurt. OK?
(*He holds out his hand.*)
JOHN: OK, sir.
SAILOR: See you around, maybe, *sailor.*
(*He strolls off, leaving them staring after him.*)

140. FILM INSERT

Yankee Doodle Dandy: *Jimmy Cagney singing and dancing Yankee Doodle.*

141. EXT. DRIVEWAY TO SCHOOL. DUSK

JOHN *and* WATSON. JOHN *is imitating Cagney, loudly.*

WATSON: Shut up, you silly sod! They'll hear you. You had too much cider in the buffet. I told you not to.

JOHN: Whoopee! I'm seeing Jenny tomorrow. You'll have to come with me. And remember, when we get in, we've been practising up in the top fields.

WATSON: Well, I don't know . . . look out, they've seen us.

VOICE: (*Calling*) Who's there?

(*They make a dash towards the school.*)

WATSON: I'm going this way.

(*They split directions.* JOHN *reaches the school and bursts into the changing-room lavatory, locking himself in. He waits, breathing heavily in a semi-drunken stupor.*)

142. EXT. SCHOOL. DUSK

The figure of the HEADMASTER. WATSON *runs right into him and is grabbed.*

HEADMASTER: Who is it? Ah – Watson. In a hurry. You're late for prep – half an hour in fact. Where have you been? Come on, don't dally. The truth, boy.

WATSON: We've . . . to the cinema, sir.

HEADMASTER: Very well. Wait outside my study.

(WATSON *goes.*)

143. INT. LAVATORY. NIGHT

JOHN *is leaning against the locked door. He peers at his watch. It is quite quiet. Slowly he unlatches the door. The* HEADMASTER *is waiting outside.*

HEADMASTER: Osborne? Looking a little unsteady I see. Where have you been? Watson has already told me.

JOHN: We've been up the top field, practising, sir. We forgot the time.

HEADMASTER: I see. Follow me.

144. INT. OUTSIDE HEADMASTER'S STUDY. NIGHT

JOHN *is waiting. Presently,* WATSON *appears, clearly in some pain.*

Pause.

WATSON: He says, go in.

JOHN: Judas!

WATSON: Joe Soap...

145. INT. HEADMASTER'S STUDY. NIGHT

JOHN *stands in front of his desk.*

HEADMASTER: You have a very great deal to learn about this
life. I begin to wonder if you ever will at all. Some of us
carry with us irredeemable flaws that no teaching or precept
can overcome. I would expel you tonight if it were not for
the fact that you should be sitting your School Certificate
next summer. Also that your mother is a widow and a hard-
working woman. You will be allowed to stay and be
confined to the school bounds till the end of the present
term when I shall come to a decision about your future. If
you have been sensible you will be allowed to remain at this
school to sit for your exam. I have here also – a packet of
letters handed to me by a prefect. I examined them
naturally and find them to be letters written to you by my
niece. They are, I suppose, in their foolish way, what you
might call 'love letters'. They *appear* to be innocent and she
refused to give me letters that she says you have written to
her. However, I have forbidden her to contact you in any
way at all. The same constraint applies to you – otherwise I
shall not hesitate to send you away on the spot. As you have
worked so hard for the concert you will be allowed to take
part in that. These kind of gestures will get you nowhere,
now or ever. I should think about it. The world is only just
outside, you know.

146. INT. HALL. NIGHT

Over the proscenium arch a banner proclaims: AID TO CHINA
FUND. JOHN *is singing in a rather faltering baritone a silly,
romantic ballad, 'The Lady from Alcazar'. He sings it with some
feeling, watched by the school and* JENNY, *who is seated beside her
uncle.*

58

147. INT. FORM ROOM. DAY

JOHN *on his own writing a letter to* MICKEY *to the ever-present
stumbling of 'Für Elise' in background.*

JOHN: (*Voice over*) 'I kept sending her notes but no answer. She
  won't even answer or look at me. I can't believe it. We
  seemed to feel exactly the same. And now they've sent her
  away. I can't believe it. I think they'll let me come back
  next term. I miss the old shelter . . .'

148. EXT. GARDEN. DAY

MICKEY *is reading the letter.*

JOHN: (*Voice over*) 'It seems even worse this term. I seem cut off
  from life, the war, everything. I can't see what's going to
  happen to me. I thought Jenny would write to me in the
  holidays at home but she didn't. Women! I was allowed out
  for the first time for half-term. Went to see a film called
  Double Indemnity with Fred Macmurray and Barbara
  Stanwyck. Wasn't allowed to go with Watson. He seems to
  keep away from me this term. Wish I knew what I was
  going to do. It's all so uncertain. I miss Jenny. All the
  Yanks have gone. We all miss them. What are the buzz
  bombs like? The news doesn't look so good. They say now
  it could go on for years. Remember that first Christmas?'
  (MICKEY *looks up. The sound of a flying bomb cutting out. He
  waits, counting, for the explosion. It comes and he stuffs the
  letter in his pocket.*)

149. FILM INSERT

Newsreel: The Normandy landings.

150. EXT. COUNTRYSIDE. DAY

Overlooking the estuary. JOHN *walking.*

JOHN: (*Voice over*) 'I go for walks on my own now when I can.
  They don't seem to take any notice of me as long as I don't
  do anything. They don't trust me. Just leave me alone. To
  make a wrong move I suppose. Sit for School Cert. on
  Monday. History in the morning. German in the
  afternoon.'

151. INT. EXAMINATION ROOM. DAY

JOHN, *with rows of other* BOYS *in silence, staring at his paper.*

JOHN: (*Voice over*) 'History wasn't too bad. Everything we'd
done. All I seem to know about England is 1688 to 1815.
Then it comes to a stop. Wish *something* would come to a
stop. German was a piece of cake.'

152. INT. EMPTY CLASSROOM. DAY

JOHN *watches a cricket match from the window.*

JOHN: (*Voice over*) 'Well, that's over. I don't know if I did well
or not. People keep saying, "What are you going to do
next?" How do I know? It's all bloody *chaos* if you ask me.
I'm kept in all the time, even though the exams are over.
The rest of the boys seem to play cricket all the time and go
on the river. Think I'll go potty . . .'

153. INT. DINING ROOM. DAY

BOYS *listening to the wireless. It is Frank Sinatra singing 'Nancy
with the laughing face', accompanied by the sound of screaming
girls.*

WATSON: What's he doing for God's sake? Taking off his
trousers!

(*The* HEADMASTER *appears and switches over peremptorily to
the BBC News – 8 May 1945. The announcer is reading that
the war in Europe is over. Uproar all round.*)

154. EXT. PLAYING FIELDS. DAY

A large group of BOYS *are dragging a piano over to a large bonfire,
led by* JOHN *delirious with excitement. The red strings snap and
twang in the summer air. He is elated for the first time for ages.*

155. FILM INSERT

Newsreel: VE Day celebrations in London.

156. INT. SCHOOL HALL. DAY

A banner hangs from the wall near the assembled BOYS. *It reads:*
'THEY GAVE ALL.'

R. BESTON. PRIVATE RAC. KILLED IN ACTION, LIBYA. APRIL 1942.
AGED 25.

H. G. BLUNT. CORPORAL RASC. KILLED IN ACTION. NORTH AFRICA.
DECEMBER 194? AGED 27.

T. L. E. MAINE. PILOT OFFICER RAF. KILLED IN ACTION. GERMANY.
FEBRUARY 1945. AGED 21.

R. H. POOLE. PILOT OFFICER RAF. MISSING, PRESUMED DEAD, THE
NORTH SEA. OCTOBER 1941. AGED 25.

R. S. EVANS. SIGNALLER KOYLI. KILLED IN ACTION. ITALY. APRIL
1944. AGED 19.

A. L. TIMSON. SERGEANT RAF. KILLED IN ACTION OVER EUROPE.
MAY 1944. AGED 20.

'AT THE GOING DOWN OF THE SUN AND IN THE MORNING, WE
WILL REMEMBER THEM.'

HEADMASTER: ... high spirits and relief at the end of this
    terrible war is one thing but wilful destruction and *anarchy*
    is another. We are here now to build a new and better
    world – not destroy the good that has been left us. I shall
    not let this matter rest and the proposed Celebration
    Holiday will not take place until I have found this *new*
    enemy in our midst. Mr Prentiss . . .
    (*They all stand and sing, 'All people that on earth do dwell'.*)

157. INT. DINING ROOM. DAY
A group of depressed-looking BOYS, *sipping evening cocoa and
listening to Glen Miller. The* HEADMASTER *passes them and
catches* JOHN's *eye, an ironic smile on his face. He loses control and
slaps his face savagely.* JOHN, *shocked and then enraged, hesitates.
Then he punches the* HEADMASTER *with all his frustrated passion.
Knocking him over the urn of cocoa and across two trestle tables.
Slowly the* HEADMASTER *picks himself up. Some* BOYS *pick up his
book and spectacles for him. He looks triumphantly across the room
at* JOHN.

158. INT. LYONS CORNER HOUSE. DAY
JOHN *watches his* MOTHER *reading a letter.*
MOTHER: '. . .as well as clandes–, cland–', what?
JOHN: Where we wouldn't be spied on.

MOTHER: '... assignations with my niece. Your son, I must
warn you...' Blimey, I knew there'd be a girl in it
somewhere. What's going to *happen* to you? I don't know.
Your father must be turning in his grave.

159. INT. PUB. NIGHT
The dance floor is packed. JOHN *watches the dancing: 'American
Patrol'. A GI jiving furiously with a* GIRL. *Through the noise he
hears his* MOTHER *calling him over.*
MOTHER: Oi! Get up them stairs! (*Shrieking*) I know – don't tell
me. Second thing he did was take his pack off! (*More
shrieks.*) Come over here and meet Eric then. (*To* ERIC)
He's not supposed to be in here. The guvnor could lose his
licence. Eric, this is my son. (*To* JOHN) Well, try and look
as if you're enjoying yourself now you are here. This is
Eric. He's been ever so good to us, with the rationing and
that. Perhaps *he* can do something with you.
ERIC: What's the matter, son? Aren't you glad it's all over?
JOHN: I don't know...
(*The noise increases.*)
ERIC: Give him a drink.

160. INT. PUB. NIGHT
JOHN *joins reluctantly in a mass hokey-cokey. His* MOTHER
shouting and laughing away opposite him.

161. EXT. CEMETERY. DAY
JOHN *and his* MOTHER *at graveside. She is tossing away old
flowers and milk bottles.*
MOTHER: Look at it. It's a bloody disgrace. We pay rates for
that. If he'd been killed in the war, I suppose they'd look
after it. Have to get yourself killed to be looked after.
JOHN: We don't pay rates.
(JOHN *looks at the small headstone. It reads:*
THOMAS GODFREY OSBORNE
BORN MAY 8TH 1900
DIED JANUARY 27TH 1940.)

GOD ROT
TUNBRIDGE WELLS

TAKING TO DEATHBED

It was always my policy, even as a small boy at Court at Weissenfels, never to wilfully fart in front of ladies. Now it is no longer of any account. I have only myself to affront. I am, yes, I am taking to my bed, my deserved and no doubt, filthy, yes, and indeed it is, oh, dear, still incaked and filthy, midden bed. Even my dearest friends would call it so and who can blame them for their kindly honesty?

My bed. It was not my intention to do so – slouch off to it – in such haste but events, and events in all such absurdity – have, for the moment, wrecked my good humour, which has, well, most will admit endured for most of a lifetime. And my good fortune, for I have *had* good fortune, and have made no secret of it.

The Wig? Discard it. Unless until such time as I can properly support it. It hides nothing that the world doesn't know or is indifferent to. I understand it's long out of fashion, old curly locks. It's all powdered perukes and pigtails with the young ones. I can't pretend to wearing *them*.

A rich hovel of a bed and who else would leap to clamber into it. To be in my own filthy, filthy bed, no angels yet at my head, but . . . So be it. And a good thing. I ask for no worse. Oh harmony, heavenly, heavenly harmony!

MESSIAH

Why? This bed? At this night, this very night, I am attending a performance of *Messiah*, my *Messiah*, if I may call it so, and I think I may. *Messiah*, given by the Tunbridge Wells Amateur Music Club. Well, an occasion and gathering of such cloud-thundering banality that, well, I would have feigned oncoming death but that it seemed so certain to be at hand that the deception would have been superfluous.

Why do I rage? Fruitless enterprise. Rage. A word I have given back to the English to puzzle over. It does no good to them or myself.

Mediocrity is a great comforter and why should I take it upon myself to deprive them of their luxury. Not from my dying bed, if that is what it's becoming. For the moment, I know not. I am too exercised by this evening's foolishness . . . Nothing will disabuse them or their kind . . . Of their silly negligence.

As for my own worth, I have always been cognizant of it, in the teeth of mercenaries and carpers. Also, I have been blessed by great magnanimity of others. I must not complain too idly.

Oh, scraps of memory. I have a 'dry' humour they tell me. Meaning that it eludes them. But this *Messiah*, what an assault upon an old man, the Old Buck, I hear they call me, Old Buck, good enough, shaken with the rack of gout (malady no man should dare smirk upon), Old Buck, ulcerated, fevered, paralysed twice if only in parts, blind these ten years, that is, not seeing, though I doubt it, any of it, gains more attention than my portliness, what they call me being large-made and awkward complexion. Impetuous, rough, peremptory, peremptory, *have* I been all that. Yes, even now. But – ill-nature – no, ill-nature, I think not. No, no. Though God may bear me down.

Ah the solicitude of harmless complaint . . . comforted in one's own filthy self.

May God rot Tunbridge Wells. Its waters and its damned sawing fiddlers. Neither have done anything but ill to me. I tried all the cures, the sulphur baths, the waters.

'Surely, you must care for your own music, Mr Handel,' they say to me. As if it had not come out of my own bowel and tripes in the first place. Their assumption might be overwhelming were it not so uncomprehending of all I had endeavoured. The ignorance of scholars or so it appears to me makes the whims of princes seem divine. I can at least be grateful to *them*.

They have called me coarse, Old Buck, Old Buck, gifted but crude, that was it, gifted but crude but what I left they called polished, polished and fully equipped. Until they get their hands to it – like Tunbridge Wells. What was I thinking about? Oh yes, farting in front of ladies. Well, God saved them – and me – from being blown into a strawberry hell of almighty commotion or something of the sorts, but, at the end, I had not the inclination nor the energy.

66

Return and return again . . . Sight goes, emotions do not grow old, and not even Doctor Sharp, great surgeon of Guy's and his hideous butchery can bring back light. And yet – the brightness – is before me each hour even if it might light up nothing. What things, such – performance. How dare they do it to me and then wheedle their way up to me for praise of all things. Praise! They should be damned for their presumptions and unloving piety.

My *Messiah*. God, what a mountainous mess they *will* make of it . . .

Behold, I show you a mystery. We shall not all sleep but we shall all be changed.

In a moment, in the twinkling of an eye, at the last trump: *for the trumpet shall sound, and the dead shall be raised*, incorruptible, and we shall be changed.

I do not think that I have been truly corruptible. I may have been, yes, have been – pagan – in spirit but I have always known there is more sincerity in religion than in politics. More truth also.

I am myself alone . . . But it only seems so. The Charming Brute. That is what they dubbed me. Charming Brute. Little charm at this present, my kind friends, wigless and eyeless.

And we shall be changed . . .

So when this corruptible shall have put on uncorruption, and this mortal shall have put on immortality, then shall be brought to pass the saying that is written, 'Death is swallowed up in victory.'

Ah yes, *Messiah, Messiah*, oh death where is thy sting? Oh grave, where is thy victory. Faith has nothing in common with certainty. Something the opinionated bladders of the spas cannot fathom. Faith, I have accepted, faith, gratefully and denied myself certainty. Fair? Surely. It stings surely enough. Wigless and eyeless. It is sin which is the sting.

But I have overmatched myself, stolen with some glory from others, above all myself. I may have borrowed from others, no, plundered, most of all myself, but I have usually repaid with considerable interest.

Sightless in Brook Street. Chide yourself by all means but not

excessively so. There is a way to go yet. Damn Milton and *his*
blindness. He also serves who only stands and waits. What stuff.
I wonder if Mr Milton was ever eyeless – certainly not in
Tunbridge Wells in an almighty din.

> 'God doth not need
> Either man's work or his own gifts. Who best
> Bear his mild yoke, they serve him best . . .'

What canting stuff. Man's work may mean little to the
burghers of Tunbridge Wells. But being eyeless in the Pantiles
is no mild yoke. Not to me. The best service I ever did to God
was my work. It was honestly executed. And by faith. *I* never
stood nor waited, not even for princes. And I see no reason to
do either for God, notwithstanding Mr Milton tugging at his
forelock to Him. No, I'd sooner be wigless as they know me in
Vauxhall and Ranelagh . . . I am repeating myself. So do all we
musicians. Like the very seasons.

HALLE

Now there was a place to remove myself from. I *became* an
Englishman; I *did*, and no one would dispute it but I never
forgot Halle or Germany. Englishness simply became me more.
It sat very nicely upon me.

London, well, I must think on that later, London; Bath, what
places, all preferable, even, oh yes most certainly, even
Tunbridge Wells to Halle, my birthplace, the Continental
courts, Berlin, Florence even.

Did I say, I did, God rot Tunbridge Wells. Oh, heaven I was
made to be churlish. I had no wish to be. So much trouble
taken, in part to please me and all wasted. It has always been
said of me that my own general look was heavy and sour and I
seemed not to know how to smile. It is most unjust but there is
no remedy. I have always smiled within. *Surely* that must be
plain enough! Arise, shine for thy light is come! I have always
felt the light, cannot they see it – even if I can no longer. No, I
exaggerate. The trumpet sounds wrongly this time. Burney,
good theatre friend, said a most sweet thing which I could not

believe at the time and now cannot forget. 'When he *did*, smile, that is, Handel, it was his sire the sun, bursting out of a black cloud.' Most others saw only the black cloud, but Burney saw the sun. 'A sudden flash which I hardly ever saw in any other.'

I have heard many such kindnesses. I endeavour not to forget them.

MY YOUTH

Halle: it was commonplace, small and pious. It would be a strange man who disclaimed his birthplace, but it was, without doubt, a flat and tedious countryside. Then Berlin, a capital city at least, Hamburg, well, the opera was 'free' and not wrapped up by the courtiers, Weissenfels, Italy. But England, England, that was the draw, the draw in trade, politics, prospects, and, most of all freedom, freedom you could sniff on the air, and that's no false trumpet sound of memory but what I know, and only I must know of my own youth and it is very clear to me, clearer, far clearer than the Amateur Musicians' *Messiah* of a few hours past.

Freedom was given up to me, here, in this countryside, in this my own foreign, my own land. I have never yet overcome its language, but I have put my own weight into it. Milton, Dryden, Congreve, I served them all, all and more and most of all, the Bible, Isaiah, Corinthians, what gifts they all have been.

> 'But – Oh, what art can teach!' Oh, indeed.
> 'What human voice can reach
> The sacred organ's praise?
> Notes inspiring Holy love
> Notes that wing their heavenly ways
> To men, to mend the choirs above!'

I can tell a tale in four languages at once but it's a dubious occupation. I can swear and eat and drink in them too, which is not such a small thing.

LONDON AND THE COUNTRYSIDE

I became, above all, it seemed a Londoner, the premier

Londoner, you might say the Laureate of that city in music that is to say, but I loved England too. Not all my time was spent here, not here in filthy bed, sightless in Brook Street. I followed the coach routes and I saw, I *saw* them, the garden of Kent, the great openness of Salisbury Plain, morning sunshine in Epping Forest, the royal antiquities of Chester, York and Durham, Hampshire the home of angling. It was manly, magnificent, deeped in the contemplation of man. I have been, yes, I am a proud man, but I have bowed down to poets, landscape, the life of the country and that of the town. I still do. There cannot be too much pride in that. I have contemplated man and his gifts and been astounded and continue to be so. It will be so always.

I have tried to be generous to the poor. I must try and be magnanimous to Tunbridge Wells. God rot it, and, blessedly, keep it.

LONDON

What an abundance, what a setting for the harmony of man it was, Vauxhall, Ranelagh, the Rotunda, the Chinese Gardens, raising us above pain, stink, corruption, humiliations, gout even, yes, the caprice of fashion, the curse of gin and its alleyways and the despair of foundlings, the blot of bankruptcy, insolvency and ill-health, surgery without relief or much hope; the whims of princes, brokers and pit-goers and theatre managers, Bishops of London or Canterbury. London, it was the centre and target of everything. May it remain so.

And then the singers . . .

SINGERS

I think, no I have, done well by singers. Only *they* might dispute it. Writing their parts has too often been like serving a puffed-up actor, bedding a plain woman out of kindliness rather than lust or lending money to the ingrate of heart. It only excites their fury and revenge. Yes, I always played fairly with them, which is more than most did, sent on their fees to whatever inconvenient place they had flown. I owed no one ever. They said I was imperious and quick to anger. It's true I did not easily brook opposition but I was fair and would always admit my error – when, but when it was demonstrated to me. Even in chiding and finding fault I tried to amuse rather than hurt. But they are unforgiving. For all the vast sums I always sent after them. They all loved money and had no reason for complaint on that score from me ever.

Singers: I swear no child, and I have I am certain none of my own to fire my feeling, child, that is to say, was as ingrate as your singer, so vain, so full of cupidity and gin cunning: Italians, Scots, Germans, mongrels; Baldassari, Durastanti, Anastasia Robinson, Mrs Turner Robinson, wife of the Westminster Abbey organist – two odd instruments. Alexander Gordon from Aberdeen, Nicolini, and, of course, Senesino who succeeded him from Dresden, Aberdeen. Senesino: castrati were not much thought of then by Englishmen but they were a draw with the women.

The worst must surely have been Cuzzoni, diminutive, ugly Venetian virago with such a regard for herself and so little for me.

I introduced her to London. It was not necessary. No one could flaunt herself with such brutal easefulness. Her and her dumpling accompanist, yes, Sardoni. 'A nest of nightingales in her belly,' they bawled from the gallery when they heard her first in my *Ottone*. They were demented for her.

Vile harridan and all at her feet. My depressed state was at its worst. Broken in health and all but without hope and penniless from my adventure in the South Sea Bubble: they, none knew, that she had refused to sing the first air in rehearsal. At last I said, 'Madam, I know that you are a veritable and a quarrelsome she-devil but, I am, I am Beelzebub.' Then I hung her out of the open window, which was conveniently open at the time, until she capitulated. Which she did. Then, it is a sorry way to go seriously about one's business and one is dismissed in one's own esteem; no matter about it now. I had no great animus toward her. Only that she was a grasping queen of such selfishness. Like all of them, she had a preposterous estimate of herself. Like most ladies. She always, I saw to it, received her preposterous fee without question. *I* had no redress. Or little enough until I took it on myself. You cannot rifle a singer's wardrobe. They must be paid. The musician's house is open to any thief. My poor copyright is unenforceable to be sure.

Poxy publishers and pirates marauding, leaky laws of copyright, so-called, what chance had I? But I tried, I tried and succeeded here and there now and then. Calling them things like *Favourite Songs*, publishing them in *The Pocket Companion for Gentlemen and Ladies*, Ladies and Gentlemen not prepared to pay that is, or, more ordinarily simply performing without pay or permission. Ah well, God rot them. It will do them no good though it's done me some damage.

I work swiftly and have always. *Messiah* in twenty-one days. There's no special merit in it nor prevaricating either. It is there and must be done. Heaven cannot wait too long for any of us and not for me. But it could do nothing when the managers decamped with the profits *I* had made them or predict the Queen's funeral and the theatres closed for mourning, the Thames freezing over, with the playhouses closed again, the outbreak of war with Spain, earthquake shocks and rumours, South Sea Bubble and my investment gone; my first performance of my *Deborah*, and could you believe it, doubling the price of tickets in an attempt to save myself, Walpole brings in his Tobacco Tax, which everyone abhors, the result of which is that my poor *Deborah* is shunned by the public, not because of me, but damn politicking, the Prime Minister and everyone's pockets except my own.

Now, if *I* stole as I did, it was from myself, unlike the warblers and politicos and the rest. Oh, why dissemble? I used the same music again and again. 'Awake the Ardour of the Breast', 'Let envy not conceal her', the *Allegro* from Concerto Grosso Number 3, I merely shifted to one of the Chandos Anthems, yes, dear *Deborah*, many, many more. They bear repeating in the right frame. Only dull readers of scores and scholars remember. I never wrote for the eye but only the grateful ear.

Cuzzoni. Who will pass on her name when I am dead? And

Faustina, Faustina her poxy adversary in *Admeto*, my success. It was my mistake to write two parts of such equal prominence. Profligacy bites the hand like the aggrieved borrower. At least my Foundlings can have no grievance against me. I shall soon be dead and a name above the door. There is little profit in the superfluity of excellence. *And* it leads the garrulous and ignorant critic to rush off searching for something to displease them. As they did with me and Buononcini. *Will* they hear of him, of Buononcini, when I have gone? But they have thought more ill of me than him and praised him.

As for – Cuzzoni and Faustina, the brawl and the faction in the Playhouse, the abuse, catcalling, like Whig against Tory, the two warbling gorgons battering the other on the stage itself, and in the presence of the Princess of Wales herself! Who will remember it? It is diminished soon enough.

ROYALS

I think I have been a convivial companion. Particularly here in England. The English are learning to be English, they see the world is theirs. Ah, Marlborough, poets and tradesmen. As well as militia, gardeners and builders of fine houses and town squares more than your politicos. And I have learnt along with them, although I have not mastered that mighty organ language like the harpsichord, and my other portable organ, no one denies my mastery, not there.

Prince Ruspoli invited me to take part in a keyboard contest with Scarlatti. There were castrati and the courtiers and, though I cannot seriously approve such idle contests, I won. I did and the applause I received was well merited and I cannot pretend I was not happy, going afterwards to hunt with hawk and horse at the Prince's invitation. Sport, pursuit, it was all as in music, all a delight. I have lived with my music as I have my friends, princes and all. I have had to make accommodation, as we do, but not so much to princes as singers.

The Elector passed over my defection to England and Queen with good humour although I was told the disgrace would ruin me. But London was tempting, oh so tempting to a young man, the young girls, little Mary Granville and those sweet children. How could I return to dull Hanover. The Princess of Wales, she was always kind to me, when the Maids of Honour chattered during my performances I not only swore at them but called out at them, anything that might come to me. And always the Princess would intervene. 'Hush,' she'd say, 'Hush. Handel's in a passion.'

Mr Handel's in a passion. As if I were ever, had ever, been out of one, whether it were desolation or idle comicality.

I have been lenient with princes and they have smiled on me, as they should have done.

But not churchmen or scribblers. Addison was bumptious and ignorant, and full of envy ... An example: an opinionated cleric approached me with such lordliness in Vauxhall: 'What wretched music they are playing here.' 'You are right, sir,' I said. 'It is very poor stuff. I thought so myself when I wrote it.'

I may have been endowed with a pagan heart, imbibing inordinately, tickling the little girls and fondling overmuch but I have given myself to God at keyboard and organ and instrument more than most men, and I tell you. I have little care for bishops, clerics and their lackeys. Bishops, presumptuous prelates, they sent me the words, mark, for my Coronation Anthems. I said: I'd forgotten more German than I'd learned English and I could rely very well on my own Bible for the making of their Anthems. And so I did. For George II we had 47 singers and 160 players. The Archbishop of Canterbury observed that it was an occasion of ceremonial rather than artistic splendour. There's the brush. The ceremony was in the splendour and the art was in both and *he* could see neither. It has long seemed to me that clerics and academics hate all art, life, literature and most surely music.

Only four years later, I was in Oxford for a series of my own concerts, which was not only most enjoyable to those who were honest or open to the gifts of this life as well as being most profitable to me. And what should happen but the famous Master of some College denounced me, in all his classical ignorance, *and* my musicians, as 'Handel and his lousy crew ... a great number of foreign fiddlers'.

74

Princes, prelates, even when tolerable, must be resisted. There are those who will not hear even the last-sounding trumpet, let alone this night. Not even music can or will shift their intransigence even in the sight of God Himself.

All the passions of the heart can be possessed in simple harmony, even without words, yes, its harmony, its unity, its order must prevail. I know it even as I am sightless, I can see. No priest or any other pestilence would make me believe otherwise.

FRIENDSHIP

But from harmony, in all this past disharmony, tattered friendships, a few, Christopher, but that will mend itself. I'll see to it. Dissembling, brazen cheating and treachery, I have known friendship and even the gift of love, at times. Although I remember when the great master organist, Buxtehude, offered me his place in Lubeck, a most important opportunity for me as the young man; I was forced to fly in the face of both friendship and admiration at the contract which bound me to marrying his grotesque and loathsome daughter. They were undertakings I could not entertain even as a *young* buck.

JEPHTHA AND BLINDNESS

My last oratorio, it turned out. Oratorio and opera, what an absurd war we made of it. What the English like is something they can beat time to. Like *Judas Maccabaeus*, which I didn't think much of. But, oh, it was very popular. Now: *Theodora*, was a favourite of mine, I did cherish that, but, well, it had a Christian subject and a tragic end. The town didn't like it at all.

Come back again to Buononcini, who will remember him? Perhaps they will, but they flocked to those simple, easily memorized melodies. *He* had the public's appeal. I always drifted to theatricality but not at the expense of truth.

Buononcini, Galuppi, Laupaugnan, *they* were the masters, they said.

There were the damned prosperous on my side and the aristocrats on theirs.

However, on my side, if it can be called so, were the Evangelicals, the Methodists and all those who truly and fundamentally hate pleasure. What allies and mercenaries. They damned *Messiah*, blasphemous they said, blasphemous, Good God that bringest glad tidings! An act of religion, unsuited to the playhouse, if you please. *Semele*: again, a strong party against it – oh, the fine ladies, *petit maîtres* and ignoramuses.

No, the opera crowd did not relish my oratorio. Once, it was so crowded and then there were the empty walls. My friends were loyal. 'Never mind,' I said. 'The music will sound the better. And if you are alone there next Friday night, I will play it to you myself.'

Jephtha: My left eye almost gone; my 66th birthday, but I felt a little better. The Old Buck is quite well. But nothing took me as long. I worked in haste, an opera in three weeks. The *Messiah* twenty-one days, twenty-one days, but then the *rest*.

> How dark, O Lord, are thy decrees.
> All hid from mortal sight!
> All our joys to sorrow turning.
> And our trumpets into mourning.
> As the night succeeds the day.
>> No certain bliss
>> No solid peace
>> We mortals know
>> On earth below
> Yet on this maxim will obey
> Whatever *is*, is right.

The *Messiah*: Now, Dublin. It *was* a triumph, the beautiful women, the Lord Lieutenant in tears and 200 more. But London, what a come-back. A Bishops' Special Convocation to denounce me. May God rot *them*. I know that *my* redeemer will redeem *me* at the last.

Blindness: Total eclipse! No sun, no moon! All dark amid the blaze of noon.

Some, they say, were driven to tears.

I will have to call on Christopher to manage my affairs and help me curb my rough tongue, the writing of letters and so on.

THE ROYAL FIREWORKS

What have I done for the Georges of England! For the Royal Fireworks, a crowd of 12,000 assembled. We had our bank of three kettledrums, three side drums, thirty wind and eighteen brass instruments. The traffic is beyond belief, nothing moves. The fireworks themselves fizzle. I cannot say I was amused. But the music *was* good. What *effort*.

WATER MUSIC

If the fireworks were a damp squib, well, the *Water Music* was an even greater dampener. We had fifty players for the first George and they sank most good humouredly. I am a fiddler from Hanover myself ... so ... It was all in good nature not so much grandeur.

MY WILL

My final codicil: to have the permission of the Dean and Chapter to be buried in Westminster Abbey in a private manner ...

Twenty thousand pounds, most earned by oratorios in the last season, my niece in Germany, £9,000 to my servants, my cook Waltz, some charities and friends ...

I give and bequeath to Mr John Smith my little house organ, my musical books and £800 ... To my servant Peter le Blond, my clothes and linen and £300 ... To my other servants a year's wages ... So often, I went to bed instead.

The Foundlings: as to my Foundlings, I was a Governor of their hospital. I hoped it might be some small remedy against gin which reduced women to depravity and their poor, condemned offspring. Seven thousand pounds I did raise with

77

Messiah for their offspring in the chapel. But then, then, they sued for exclusive, exclusive, mark you, rights in it. I stopped them but they shall have a copy of the score.

Bald, blind and crippled already and that's a long time ago. It seems so. Paralytic disorder in the head. Lady Shaftesbury was kindly.

LADY SHAFTESBURY: It was such a melancholy pleasure, as drew tears of sorrow to see the great though unhappy Handel, dejected, wan and dark, sitting by, not playing on the harpsichord, and to think how his light had been spent by *being overplied in music's cause*.

Messiah: Dear God, the new massive, modish scoring, the people I did bring Kings to their feet, but their hirelings; the blind may open their eyes, I have done my best and assisted, if only a little, in giving to the Englishman his glorious, glorious, unquenchable religion. There will be none like it. The rest, like Buononcini – will surely, must be last . . .

RAGE

I contrived at being lively, no, not contrived. I was, I think most certainly, lively myself. Just as I exercised my rage, the height of passion, there is also the clamour of peace. It will come. I know of it.

THE END

I got to England, as I swore I would, on my own bottom, but, as for heaven, ah, the diapason closing in on man . . . the compass of notes it ran.

I know not . . . we know not, but the trumpet must *surely* sound, it must, it does, I have heart, *I* have put it down, myself; on high.

> The trumpet shall it shall be heard on high
> The dead shall live; the living die
> And music shall *untune* the sky!